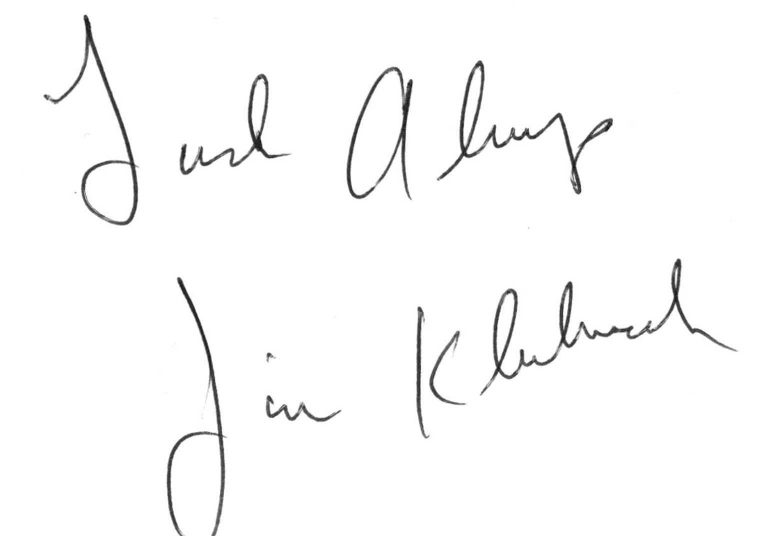

427

The Zest (and best) of Klobuchar

A lively safari into
the rollicking world of

JIM KLOBUCHAR

Popular Columnist for

This book is for my loved ones,
my creditors and my attorneys.

Copyright 1967 by the
MINNEAPOLIS STAR AND TRIBUNE COMPANY

Library of Congress Catalog Card Number 67-31458

Published by Mark Zelenovich, Inc.
Printed by The Colwell Press, Inc.

Foreword

It is a stress for any newspaperman to find an honorable, much less believable, excuse for reconstructing some of his old carpentry and thus subjecting readers to a form of double jeopardy. The fairest observation I can think of is that this little volume has been compiled not so much as a service to posterity as a favor to my bill collectors.

In addition to this there is an inviolate custom – in the peddling of vintage treads of this sort – to assure the reader of the author's level-headed view of history, his humility and the fact that his arm had to be wrenched to permit re-publication of his material.

All of this, of course, is indisputably true.

Also true is the professional axiom that whatever merit was in the original depended largely on the environment and time in which it was written – the spontaneous teeth-gnashings, the joys, the unclassified aggravations and the second-guessing omniscience that only the Monday-after can bring to the football hysteria.

And yet some of it is being presented here again on the chance that it may re-light for some a spark of the passion or the frustration of the time, or to freshly expose to others one man's scanning of the befuddling world around us. Most of it deals with the fun and fractures of life in Minnesota and the Twin Cities. On the encouragement and tolerant expense-account policies of The Minneapolis Star, however, I have spent some time abroad on what have been called misguided tours of Europe and the American west.

As a newspaper columnist, I have found life at its most comfortable when working in an atmosphere of lightfooted strife. In this the harpoons are tossed and ducked with the mutual understanding that most of it is without live ammunition and almost all of it is without malice. There are things, of course, about which one feels more strongly, and I don't think there will be any difficulty in the identification of those.

This book includes material that has appeared both in a regular column of The Minneapolis Star and in its news pages. My less charitable acquaintances advise me there are times when the columns and the news page stories are indistinguishable, and with some of this — dealing with my personal disasters primarily — I do not necessarily disagree.

As an operating rule of thumb, you can identify the column material by length if nothing else. Most of it has rather symmetric dimensions typographically if not logically, and fills almost exactly two pages in each case.

Some have asked why a newspaper columnist would risk opinions from time to time that seem to disagree with those of his publisher. To this I must say the Cowles publications do maintain a generous attitude toward heresy; and further, that while this maverick-concept of journalism may not necessarily be wise, at least it makes the job suspenseful.

The final requisite in teasing or nudging others is that you must do it to yourself and your own sacred cows enough for almost all to get the point. This I have sought to do at random times, having long ago surrendered to the intimate truth that all of us are very, very fallible. I grant that in some cases it may be a contest.

— Jim Klobuchar

Table of Contents

Calvin Soothes the Angry Skies

With hypnotized horror, I watched the Twins' field crew wheel two of those little landscaping cannons onto the sodden infield Friday. At length I blurted to my partners, "Migawd, Calvin is going to shoot the people who are leaving."

It was an unworthy thought, I know now, and the little flame-throwers were simply part of Calvin's Merlinesque arsenal of stage props, serving the same purpose as a top hat and a cane for the road-show magician.

For years people have marveled at the peculiar alchemy with which Calvin Griffith turns cloud banks into bank deposits. Yet few have been so favored as the 21,000 who yesterday witnessed an in-person performance of Griffith's art, a public spectacle as rare as the appearance of Haley's Comet or a total eclipse of the sun.

He should have had a bigger audience, and I know it wounded Calvin's creative pride that he did not, although the man is a good trouper and did not blame the authors. In the end, he won his reward. Calvin made more money stuffing sausage and popcorn into the mouths of idling spectators during the one-hour delay than he would have made selling 3,000 extra tickets.

I never had any doubt, of course, that Calvin would get the opening game started despite all the rain. My only question was: Will the game ever end?

Over the years, the fan's faith in Calvin's ability to control the weather has become proverbial, like the child's devotion to his tooth angel or the confidence of the Nicollet Mall builders in their psychiatrists.

The sky was lurid and hostile, and cataracts were roaring down the curbs. Yet there were happy thoughts in the minds of my confederates as well as foam on their noses. "Calvin," one confided, "will take care of his people."

Still, I was not so sure. Seeking reassurance, I threaded my way among the other free-loaders in the Twins room and confronted one of Calvin's favorite relatives, Jimmy Robertson.

"You think the old man has his stuff today?" I asked.

"Man," Robertson said, "I'll tell you something. People around here have come to expect a lot of Calvin. He got rid of snowbanks one year with helicopters and built a raft to get Battey from first to second another year.

"But it's his greatest challenge today. It's been raining steady for more than one hour. You know it's the people I'm thinking about, not our own petty, unnecessary profits."

"But they are sitting out there in the damp cold," I objected. "Some have taken refuge in the corridors, and it is congested there, besides which the footing is bad."

"But they are closer to our concession stands there," Robertson explained, "and nourishment is only an arm's length away."

There was so much water on the field, they were measuring the foul-line distances in nautical miles. But suddenly, there he was, Calvin, emerging on the dugout gangplank with his hat, cigarette holder and smudge pots.

Calvin stood silent and erect, gazing first at the western sky and then into the stands, where faint-hearted fans were scurrying and groveling for cover against the slanting rain.

Calvin was motionless, the image of a tempered and unbudgeable strength, of a calm and timeless nobility. One's thoughts reached for the historic symbols of stability—the Rock of Gibraltar, the Sphinx, Twin City Federal.

Now he was gazing skyward again, and the fans understood what he would try to do. Their eyes never left him. He was Farragut at New Orleans, Dewey at Manila, Noah in the park.

Slowly, almost imperceptibly, Calvin raised his right arm and with his left signaled the organ player to grind a few bars of "Let a Smile Be Your Umbrella."

And yes, the rain was stopping. Scudding clouds shifted in mid-scud. Calvin gestured again, and here came the hip-booted groundsmen breast-stroking in formation from the right-field docking area.

They reached Calvin with the benefit of a favoring tide and treaded in place there while the concession peddlers returned to their stations.

It was an astonishing performance, dimming even the Twins' victory and the game of hide-the-freeways that followed.

Having tamed the Met, Calvin next week is going to try the Red Sea.

Fats Wins by Forfeit

Normally, in the annual Thanksgiving Day struggle in the dining room, I bet on the turkey as opposed to the diner.

The theory here is that while the diner may display some early speed and mobility, eventually he is going to be dragged down from behind by the turkey's superior staying power, which averages from a week to 10 days.

I am making no wagers this week, however, because the world's most caloric pool player, Minnesota Fats, is back in town for a weekend of hustling and sentimental gorging at the scene of his most spectacular triumphs as a gourmand.

"Everytime I remember those roast-beef blowouts on Hennepin Avenue 30, 40 years ago, it makes me choke up," Fats said. "They call me Minnesota Fats, but I been everywhere and it coulda been Toledo Fats or Vegetable Fats but it don't matter none because you put food on the table anywhere, man, and it's home to me."

I intercepted Fats with a telephone call to Kenosha, Wisconsin. He was en route to exhibitions in La Crosse and the Twin Cities, where he plans to show—for the benefit of Montgomery Ward hustlers—how he beat Paul Newman in the movies years ago.

Fats plans to eat Thanksgiving Day dinner in the Sheraton-Ritz, where he is going to be the only guest who has reserved a kitchen instead of a room.

"I mean when I eat in a restaurant, friend," he said, "I don't order turkey wings or legs or neck or stuffing. When I order turkey I mean a turkey, a whole one, and they better be ready because if I got too far to go on the elevator I'm gonna stop for hamburgers because brother it don't matter what it is or how it's cooked just so it's available.

"You say you got big turkeys in Minnesota but that don't scare me. I take them one at a time. I been in big-stake pool games and big-stake eating contests, and I never lost in my life. As a eater my timing's off today because I ain't slept for five days. I been to New York and some jerk wanted to put me in a tuxedo.

"Now I got 900 suits, brother, and they go up to $500 apiece but I wore a tuxedo only once in my life, for a big pool game. I been snookered, stymied and cheated in my life but this is the first time they tried to choke me."

I inquired whether Fats had ever dieted.

"Now, you got to be some kind of oddball or subversive, what they call," Fats seethed. "Who the hell ever heard of Minnesota Slats. I weigh 260, from which there ain't much deviation, and which is more or less my playing weight. I'll eat seven meals a day if I get up early enough and what I ain't got time to eat I take home to my mutt Fuzzy in a doggy bag, which we split."

Fats' achievements as one of the world's heroic trenchermen have led him to marathon combats with envious challengers the world over. Years ago he vanquished an opponent by eating a 12-pound turkey and three steaks at one sitting.

"Fats," his exhausted rival said, "I've had it. You win. But you mean you're gonna keep on eating?"

"Man," Fats said scornfully, "I'm gonna eat this steak, and then I'm gonna eat that shortcake, and if you don't get the hell outa here I'm gonna start on you."

Being contentious, I am now searching these communities for a worthy sparring partner for Fats. The name of a St. Paul newspaperman, my old running mate Roger Rosenblum, suggests itself.

Rosenblum and I used to travel with the Vikings, customarily celebrating the night before the games because there just wasn't much provocation in those days to do it after the games. In Detroit one night, Rosenblum opened the dinner uneventfully with three fishbowl martinis, graduated effortlessly to two dozen blue-point oysters, shifted to green salad and by now had gained full momentum with a $7 steak.

Having picked up the tab for Roger now and then, I bowed out urgently and left Rosenblum in the hands of Herb Carneal and others. Carneal by now was being snowed under by flying bread crumbs. The tinkle of silverware around the table had stopped. It was a virtuoso exhibition. Waiters stood around, awed, their arm towels at halfstaff. They brought Rosenblum cheesecake for dessert, and I don't mean a wedge or a square, I mean **a** cheesecake.

Shaken, a Look magazine man telephoned Toots Shor's restaurant in New York. "Shor," he said, "I've found him. The champ. All you got back there is snackers. This guy might eat the fork, too, but he's got class. He'll only go for sterling."

Defeat on Devil's Tower

He was tall and bald-headed, with a florid face and alert movements, 54 years old, but enormously strong.

Lashed to the mountain above a 70-foot vertical chute, he looped a belay rope around his body and shouted to the climber grappling with the granite column below him.

"A few feet above you there's a three-inch foothold," John Peterson said. "Jam your way up there and you can rest."

The whipping breeze had died. The advancing overcast routed the sun, and the fluted pillars of the Devil's Tower were a hostile grey.

Freezing raindrops bounced randomly off the tower walls. But the rock was still dry and climbable.

From the autumn-browned valley of the Belle Fourche River came the sounds of cattle and an unhurried automobile.

On another day it might have been an hour for meditative nature-watching but my left boot kept slipping out of the column crack and I wedged my right elbow into the thin chimney on the other side for more friction.

The pitch was perpendicular, yet Peterson had beaten it by bellying up the humped column, toeing into the fissures on either side to gain altitude and hammering pitons for protection as he rose.

He is a cautious, skilled climber, but marble-sized pebbles, dislodged as he forced the chute, showered on my plastic helmet.

"Stay left on your stance," Peterson said. "This is where a big one came down on me on Memorial Day."

He had suffered a broken hand on that day and been forced to retreat from his first attempt on the tower. He had made it to the summit on his second attempt three months later.

The Devil's Tower is a geological freak, a volcanic upthrust nearly 1,000 feet high rising as a lonely, flat-topped chimney above the rolling northeastern Wyoming grazing land and arbors of pines on the western flanks of the Black Hills.

The smooth, geological symmetry of its vertical columns makes it appear inviolable. It has the bearing of a vast, prehistoric monument which seems to suggest to today's passerby, "Look, but stay distant."

Yet it has been climbed many times since mountaineers first discovered it — never without a struggle, however, or without the ironmongery of pitons, carabiners and expansion bolts that can preserve a man when his fingertips fail and his toeholds give out.

I am not an expert mountaineer, but I had climbed enough in the Teton Mountains and Switzerland to qualify for an attempt at the tower.

Alongside Devil's Tower, the Matterhorn was a stroll on the beach. Peterson was ready for it. I wasn't. Peterson had climbed the North Face of the Grand, the ultimate classic climb in the Tetons, and he had done it by refusing to act his age.

At 54 a man has a right to a rocking chair at 5 p.m. Peterson spends his before-dinner hour walking around Lake Harriet with a 67-pound load of concrete on his back to stay in condition.

We stuffed some foul weather gear and a sandwich into our rucksacks in the morning and scrambled up the big-bouldered talus slopes at the foot of the tower.

The wind sang through the scrubby pines on the curving lower slopes of the mountain. We climbed an open-book pitch, a high-angled trough leading to a formation called the broken column, technically the most difficult stretch on the Durrance route we were attempting.

"It's strenuous above here," he said, "but if we can lick this one we're on our way."

Twenty minutes later he was standing atop a three-foot ledge that marks the end of the severe pitch.

I wedged myself up the narrow crack, got to a stance halfway up and then pried the rest of the way with my back braced against one wall and my legs jamming against the opposite face of the chimney.

I reached Peterson's stance and dropped belly-down on the little flat platform.

He was staring up at the 70-foot chute, picking out a route. His pitons and carabiners jingled at his waist as he began thrusting up the column.

"It's over," he said,"when we get up this one. Just a few grunts and scrambles from there."

Fifteen minutes later he called down for me to start climbing.

For 20 feet I went strongly, spreadeagling without much discomfort. Streamers of thin cloud were breaking against the summit approaches above us but the weather was holding so far.

I reached for a jam hold with my right hand but my left foot wasn't holding. I tried to chimney up as I had on the earlier pitch but that wasn't the technique here. I jammed my elbow into the crack on the right again and tried to pull myself up with my arms but the strength was going out of them.

I came off and fell two feet before Peterson's belay rope held me.

"Try to Prussik your way up," he called down. Peterson lowered a small looped sling and I knotted it around the belay rope, which is the climber's lifeline. I stepped into the sling and tried to raise myself that way but I needed my arms to do it, and they were numb by now.

I banged my helmet against the rock and told Peterson, "All right, let the invalid down."

I asked him to keep going to the top but we remembered the park rangers' prohibition against solo climbing. Rain was raking the tower wall and we got out rappel slings and spent an hour roping down.

Peterson looked thoughtful.

"No need to apologize on this mountain," he said. "A man goes as far as he can without breaking his neck."

"By the way," Peterson grinned, "what was it your pal Van Brocklin said when he resigned?"

"The guy said he couldn't get over the hump," I said. "We're going to form a duet."

Next spring again?

Why not?

Barbara of the Bottomless Curiosity

Barbara Flanagan's first office chore each morning – after she has finished her daily conference with the architects and redesigned the Minneapolis loop again – is to read the sports pages.

Miss Flanagan first reads the sports pages to herself and then to me, which admittedly constitutes a kind of double jeopardy to the wage earners around us.

I consider it an ideal arrangement, however, because it gives me an opportunity to gather the events of the previous day in an attitude of repose and calm deliberation.

Miss Flanagan reads with professional style and animation, a throwback to the days when she read the comic strips on radio before she got pre-empted by the Hamm's commercials.

I forgive her a slight tendency to up-tempo when she gets to names like Koufax, Killebrew, Van Brocklin and Flatley. Miss Flanagan just happens to be captivated by important people. As a matter of fact, she is the only person I know who talks in bold-face type.

The trouble is, the lady has a bottomless curiosity. I accept that this may be an ungallant term, but you must understand that I have just had a very trying interrogation at the hands of Miss Flanagan, more nerve-rattling than on most days.

Miss Flanagan asks questions, remorselessly and breathlessly, about batting averages and earned run averages. These she subdivides into batting averages against left and right-handed pitchers, earned run averages in Fenway Park and Glacier Park.

Occasionally, she asks questions that go to the very marrow of the baseball establishment. Two days ago she wanted to know what the Twins say to each other in the club sauna after a tough ball-game.

"I have been to the Twins' sauna only twice," I replied. "To the best of my knowledge the only conversation came from a fogged-in infielder who shouted, 'Turn down the damn steam, you left-handed lobster.' "

I realized this was inadequate to the lady's purposes, but I never took a tape recorder into a sauna and if Miss Flanagan wants to know what goes on in there she can go out and get her own sauna pass.

But I have to admire her persistence and so I made a stumbling effort yesterday to share my limited knowledge.

"If you compare a baseball race with a horse race like many do," she began, "are the fourth-place Twins in a good position today?"

"No."

"Well, then where would be the ideal position for the Twins at this stage of the race?"

"I would say first place."

"But if they can't be there, what would be the ideal position?"

"I would say second place."

"All right, but if you compare a baseball race with a military campaign, when would be a good time for a team to start its big push?"

"At its very earliest convenience, such as opening day."

"Is Sam Mele or Cal Griffith managing the Twins?"

"I would say right now it's a tie, but Calvin has the last at-bats and would have to be considered the favorite in extra innings."

"I notice that your old friend, Norm Van Brocklin, is quoted as saying the new football merger might bring a few more idiots into the league. What does he mean by that?"

"The last time I tried to interpret the Dutchman we ended up not talking for three weeks, which was a boon to both parties. I suppose my old friend is trying to say that whenever you bring nine new administrators into football, the law of probability takes over and some of them are bound to be squirrels."

"Isn't there now a chance of a coaching confrontation between the Dutchman and Sid Gillman of San Diego? Didn't they have some trouble when Norman was playing for the Rams and Gillman was coaching?"

"Yes, but there again, it was a standoff. Gillman considered Van Brocklin abnormal and Van Brocklin considered Gillman subnormal."

Cowpoke's Lament

THE J-R BAR, JACKSON HOLE, WYO. – He wore a Stetson hat and a 90-proof blush on his cheeks that suggested he had spent more time in front of the bar than behind the hitching post in the last few years.

He appeared to be in his 70's but his manner was lean, tart, and thirsty. Indisputably, he was an old cowboy. It did not show on his boots, which were innocent of the aromatic memorabilia of the corral, but it did show in the practiced urgency with which he ordered a double shot.

He was, in short, a nugget here among the dudes, shopkeepers and guitar-plucking hippie deadbeats you will encounter in the typical western tourist town.

I caught his attention and raised my hand to him unobtrusively. "Come over and set," I drawled, "a spell."

Joe Madden nodded and, as the expression goes, sauntered over. There is simply no other way a respectable old cowboy can navigate. You and I may walk, run, waddle, or lurch. But an old cowhand, if he's worth his bedroll, will saunter.

"I've been coming to Jackson for more than 10 years," I explained, "and have been aching to talk to somebody who can give me a kind of backsage view of the Old West. All I know about cow punching I learned from Dale Evans, which is bad, and Gene Autry, which is even worse."

Madden's hands fumbled impatiently on the bar, as though groping for some lost possession. Jack the bartender smoothly rescued the situation by pouring Joe's chaser, a glass of beer.

"That's the difference between the West and the East," Madden scowled.

"How's that?" I asked.

"Out here when a guy wants some booze, he lays down some money. Out there when he wants some booze he starts a riot."

"You mentioned the movies," he continued. "I never watch cowboy movies. They ain't got it right yet. You remember 30 years ago. The cowboy was so pure he was more interested makin' love to his horse than the dame. Nowadays the guy no more'n saddles up and he's got her under the nearest cottonwood, I mean the dame. Fella, nobody out in the Old West was that fast or that good unless the two of them was doin' business.

"Me, I was born in Van Buren County, Iowa, and left when I was a kid. Why? Just to get out of Iowa. What the hell better reason you need?

"Before 1915 I was riding range out here in Wyoming for the 2-Bar Ranch. Was it big? I rode for a month without seein' a fence. You got outa your bedroll at the crack of dawn and the chuck wagon was there servin' you steak for breakfast. I used to ride down four horses a day. They paid you $1 a day, 30 bucks a month. I got an extra $5 takin' the rough-string, which were the horses nobody else wanted to ride. Five bucks extra a month for the privilege of gettin' your tail end wore off.

"I laugh at the cowboy today. He goes out into the pasture with his Ford pickup, leaves some salt, blows his horn and the cattle come runnin'.

"We ate steak three times a day, plus lousy potatoes. Every time food ran short we threw a rope around the best beef there was. Sure we ate sourdough pancakes. What the hell you think we were, dudes?"

My eyes moistened at the image of silhouetted cowpokes in twilight on the trail, gathered about the campfire mingling their strong, weathered baritones in "Ridin' Down the Canyon."

"Fella, you run down four horses a day and the first thing you're gonna do at night is crawl into your roll. Oh, we had a banjo picker around now and then but he never had a 75-voice chorus around the fire like Roy Rogers. Yes, I carried a gun, for rattlesnakes, mostly. We'd shoot each other's heels off when drunk, but not often when angry.

"Love life? The eager ones used to go to Cheyenne for the whores. The lucky and good lookin' ones found a schoolteacher. Me? I went thataway!"

In the lowering haze of the J-R Bar it was hard to tell which way old Joe was pointing.

Terror on the Way to the Forum

Before Jim Klobuchar left for Europe, Star City Editor Lee Canning advised him — in all good will and fraternity — not to risk driving in the traffic of Rome. Canning was so alarmed by the possible consequences, in fact, that he considered notifying the Italian carabinieri to keep Klobuchar off the streets. The message never was sent, Canning being tied up paying for Klobuchar's last batch of parking tickets in Minneapolis. The editor later received the following letter:

ROME, Italy — Canning:

You are not going to believe what happened to me on the way to the Forum last night.

In the United States I have driven freeways, alleys, speedways, one-way streets, wrong-way streets, sidewalks and catwalks. I have been badgered by road hogs, speed traps, women drivers, chuckholes and manholes.

None of this, however, prepared me for the unrelieved terror of last night, and I want to apologize to you publicly. I should not have gone near the stradas without escort or anti-tank armament.

Disregard the fact that I got lost on the way to the Forum, not once but five times. The Forum is a hard place to miss. It is in the heart of this lovely but volcanic city and is the place where almost all roads lead over one bridge or another.

When driving, you do not need a compass to find the Forum, but you do need a lot of luck.

Roman drivers, as a matter of national character, move at high velocity and cross-purposes. There is no such thing as a right-of-way. Dawdlers are either flattened or blind-sided into the Tiber River.

The first two hours are the most grueling. Natives will tell you that if the novice Roman driver survives the first two hours he has a fighting chance of making it through the night.

The catacombs, you hear it whispered, are full of the bones of complacent California tourists who thought they knew something about defensive driving in Los Angeles.

In Rome, you cannot survive with a defensive mentality. You must go onto the attack from the moment you slip into your Fiat, and you must maintain that posture of pugnacity wherever the road leads. If you make a mistake, they build a monument out of you and you are thus immortalized.

But I survived, and I owe it to my quick adaptation to the unique style of Roman driving which might be classified as unregulated, one-way weave.

To the newcomer, Roman drivers appear to be steering on faith, with a destination determined mainly by hope. Because of the profusion of squares, fountains, churches and expresso hangouts, the traffic tends to move in concentric circles. To make time, drivers look for the grooved lanes in the fashion of a 500-mile racer at Indy.

Consequently, the driver who gets trapped in the inside lane moving around the Colosseum, for example, is doomed to travel in circles indefinitely until he either runs out of fuel or is embolded to try to crash out.

I saw one inexperienced driver attempt this second maneuver and fail. I looked back sadly on the demolition scene, and last saw the driver sharing a platform with a marbleized emperor from the second century.

I suppose I could have managed Rome well enough without an automobile. But I had this letter of introduction in my pocket, and I simply had to discover the truth.

Shortly before I left the states I learned there was no rent-a-car credit card in my portfolio and, assuming the largest of the car rental agencies would be the logical choice for this, I called the Hertz people asking for some kind of emergency accreditation. I tried four different ways to give Hertz my business. But I never got past the small print lawyers in the company's offices, who insisted I would need two weeks to be authorized.

I didn't call Avis, on the theory that Avis would be breathing too hard from chasing Hertz and would be in no position to talk. I then telephoned National Car Rental, and explained my predicament.

"National," announced one of its Chicago managers, "may be No. 3 in sales, but always keeps its customers squarely where they belong. You will have a letter of introduction waiting for you at the airport, to present to our people in Zurich."

Only an organization based in Edina could shear away the red tape and technicalities with such dispatch and sense of comradeship.

I drove a National car in Switzerland, but switched to Avis in Rome because the hotel concierge had never heard of National and neither, apparently, had the telephone directory. I explained my problem to Avis in Rome.

The man behind the counter had the grooming and fatherly disposition of Adolph Menjou.

"Yes, we will bill you on the basis of this letter, by all means," he said, but then, viewing me solemnly, added: "You want to drive around today in Rome. Are you absolutely certain you have prepared yourself?"

I blanched at this. "Do you mean have I received last rites . . ." I started to say. He interrupted, smiling the ageless Roman smile of tolerance. "Ah, no, I mean do you know about the floor shift, and all about our illustrated street signs. But most of all, are you sure you know what you are doing?"

It had gone too far for any weasling retreat at this point, and so I got the comfortable little Fiat going.

There was an intimate sense of excitement in the first turn around the Vittorio Emanuel monument, reminiscent of my first flying solo and the first day of Army obstacle course training under live ammunition.

You do not simply enter Roman traffic, especially around a square. You first have to build up enough ground speed to stay with the flow and then dart into the pattern with flaps up and horn blowing. There is no other way.

I never did look at the speedometer. The maximum speed in Roman traffic allegedly is 31 miles an hour, but the pedestrians have to go faster than that to avoid being trampled.

The only thing with which I can compare the phenomenon is to imagine yourself driving through Seven Corners at Highway 494 speeds, moving eight cars abreast.

The Italian native's sunbeam disposition is a thing of proverb but behind the wheel of these toonerville automobiles he is a raging ogre and a friend to no man, a single-minded warrior galloping on four cylinders.

In this town, A. J. Foyt would be elected mayor. Rome is the only place in the world where drivers make pit stops instead of fuel stops.

Being unable to map-read and drive simultaneously, I used the Vittorio Emanuel monument as an orientation point, making quick forays toward the Fountain of Treve, the Via Veneto, the Colosseum, St. Peter's, and other sites in this imperishable city.

Somewhere along the route I discovered I did not know how to back up the machine. I did not communicate verbally with a taxi driver from whom I sought help, and instead I tried the standard Italian method of doing it with my hands and pursed lips.

The driver thought I wanted to fight.

Finally, I tried some pigeon Italian and said something like, "per favore, dove c'e shift in reversio."

"Shove it," he said calmly in English, "into the lower right hand corner of the gear box."

Ultimately I did make the Forum, at about 11:45 p.m., and had the uneasy sensation that even Nero had turned off the late show by then. You should probably know that I ran a red light, unavoidably, when it was a choice of going through the intersection or being forefendered into a fruit stand by one of the hornblowers behind me.

The city was magnificent, all right, but at the moment it was one big pain in the piazza.

A cop chewed me out at the curb, but wound up asking if I knew his nephew in the Bronx.

And so I parked the car at the railroad station, oblivious to the narrowness of my escape in that stampede of automobiles until I viewed the traffic from the sidewalk, and then I began to quiver. They were coming around the corner at four different angles, ready to sweep upfield, and I am mortally certain that this is where the famed Green Bay Lombardi sweep originated.

When I got back to the station I found a police officer at my windshield, writing a parking ticket. Noting my cornbelt accent, he tore up the ticket. Just a good Giuseppi.

I am heading for Venice, friend, where they drive on water.

Teddy Breaks Up the Party

Teddy Kennedy materialized in the Radisson Hotel Friday night, looking adolescent, unbeatable, and vaguely immortal.

He was preceded by Senator Fritz Mondale, who was functioning yesterday as a type of foul-weather Sir Walter Raleigh. Teddy doesn't need a Raleigh – or a coat. It was pouring outside, but Kennedy doesn't walk through or around puddles. Teddy, of course, walks on them.

He hove in view majestically at about 10 p.m. with entourage, a bonus entry in the Minnesota Press Club's Candidates Night – an occasion which, taken purely as an artistic achievement, lay somewhere between a Katzenjammer boat drill and an auction at a parrot show.

Kennedy's presence redeemed the whole thing, however. I saw Republican functionaries' wives who were ready to disown their party when Kennedy mingled with the crowd, offering benedictory handshakes.

I didn't shake hands with Kennedy. It wasn't that Mondale kept getting in the way. The most formidable obstacle was Robert Forsythe, the Republican candidate who wants to shoot Mondale out of the saddle.

Forsythe managed one of the smaller miracles of the evening, getting photographed with Kennedy at least as many times as Mondale and out-shaking Mondale with Kennedy, 3 to 2.

It got so bad Forsythe walked out of the joint saying we've just got to do something about Castro and Cuber.

For all of that, I have to acknowledge that Forsythe is my kind of candidate, and probably would win a straight head-to-head battle on the stump if Mondale didn't have a galloping lead in the polls and General Motors to throw harpoons at.

Forsythe is the Republican who is pleading poverty. "When we start talking about that $2,000 contribution from (American) Allied Insurance to the Democrats," he says, "and my friends ask me, well, what would you do with $2,000 like that, I say 'Just try me, friend, try me.'

"I'm glad to see my friends the Kennedys come in here. It gives this campaign some class. Besides, the voters now get the chance to compare the coffee-sippers like me with the tea-sippers like Teddy."

"What you are sipping now," I observed, "looks suspiciously

like bourbon."

"True," Forsythe said. "I can't afford Scotch."

The unsettling thing about Forsythe as a Republican is that he behaves like a Democrat. Without asking anybody, I got the hazy impression that he would be more comfortable running with DFLer Karl Rolvaag than Republican Harold LeVander, who, for all of his qualifications, comes on remotely like an endorsed saint running for canonization.

LeVander left the rumpus early last night. Rolvaag arrived late and left quickly, seemingly less afraid of LeVander than of blowing an appointment to meet his wife for the last half of the symphony opening.

The only one who wasn't there was William Youngdahl, the presumed DFL candidate for railroad commissioner who I understand is in the process of being exiled by the party which wanted to let the people decide. What I want to know is, since when did the Democrats get so choosy?

It didn't take long, however, for the Republicans to reveal their own problems. One of them, clearly, is going to be Robert E. Short, the DFL candidate for lieutenant-governor.

Short is one of those accomplished talkers who, when you ask him for a light, will tell you how to build a furnace.

Kennedy, Mondale, and Rolvaag bucked it to Short to hold the forensic fort at the Radisson last night after they left for more pressing business, and Short talked so eloquently he nearly got the blowout shifted to the Leamington, which is Short's favorite charity.

Short's opponent, Jim Goetz, is a young radio executive and, I'm sure, an able man. Simply from the standpoint of sustained volume last night, however, it was a little like matching Walter Cronkite against the station-break man. My view is that Short-and-Goetz will make one of the more fascinating roadshows of the campaign and probably lead the race in decibels.

Finally, my sympathies go to William Hathaway, a round and convivial college professor who may have been born under some dark star. Hathaway is running against Don Fraser for Congress. Last night he had to follow Kennedy on the rostrum. I have a feeling, also, that he had a picnic planned for today's rainstorm.

The Dragon vs. a Scrambling St. George

GREEN BAY, Wisconsin — Like Marley's Ghost in a camel-hair coat, he fulminated on the sidelines, fists beating the air, while non-immortals in the stadium quailed.

The image of Vince Lombardi in mid-fury in Green Bay was so terrifying it appeared for a moment the officials were going to cede him the island of Sicily as a gesture of conciliation.

Lombardi is the Green Bay Packer coach and as such has authority to tell the leaves when to fall and the officials when to drop their laundry in Green Bay.

Lombardi is tough enough to make Julius Caesar call for a fair catch.

But Sunday along came Francis Tarkenton of the Minnesota Vikings, and it was St. George versus the dragon all over again.

This is one of the recurring morality plays of the National Football League. Lombardi, as the ranking field marshal in the NFL, annually designs a defensive plan of exquisite beauty and resourceful scope, all intended to stop the Viking offense.

Tarkenton immediately scrambles it into a misshapen ruin, like a mischievous kid tumbling sand castles at the beach. This offends Lombardi's esthetic sensitivity and at times, like Sunday afternoon, wins the ball game for the Vikings.

But rarely do they meet head-to-head as they did Sunday in the pale yellow light of the NFL's version of the late show.

With the Vikings on offense in the first half, somebody dropped a penalty flag. Confusion overtook the officials.

"No. 77 is downfield," one of them howled.

Lombardi demanded a march-off against the Vikings. An official edged tentatively toward the Packer bench, but, not having received formal permission to address the coach, did not immediately speak.

Lombardi gestured toward the Viking goal line. The officials picked up the ball.

Tarkenton ran to them screaming.

"Who was downfield?" he demanded of an official.

"No. 77," somebody said.

"That guy," Tarkenton explained, "is wearing a green shirt. He belongs to the Packers. He can stay downfield all he wants. We're the guys on offense, and our No. 77 (Gary Larsen) is on the bench.

"Are you guys running the ball game or is Lombardi?"

Time elapsed agonizingly while everybody pondered the question. They finally bowed to the purity of Tarkenton's logic and let the play stand up.

It was one of those games, of course, which would have had everything if they had allowed the clock custodian a few more minutes at the controls. As it was, he nearly spilled into Ed Sullivan's time.

In the process he added a new dimension to the NFL's cast of characters, the scrambling timekeeper.

He got the usual inspiration from Tarkenton, who delivered the crucial play by running the Packer pursuit into the air-blowers and then waving to Jim Phillips before throwing. When Tarkenton waves once, it means the receiver should reverse field. When he waves twice, it means the receiver should run another 15 yards, cut between the tarpaulin and Gate 5, and come back toward the goal posts.

To Phillips, he waved four times, the maximum emergency wave.

"I already had run north, east, west and south," Phillips explained. "If he waved one more time I would have taken the river."

When it was over, Lombardi sat in his office, astonishingly controlled and forgiving. He was thoughtful and cordial to visitors, but you shuddered to think about the fate of the Packer defensive line on Tuesday.

He walked over to Norm Van Brocklin and addressed him pleasantly. Normally, when Van Brocklin and Lombardi meet, they hold their hands near their belts like Jack Palance and keep the wall behind them.

Van Brocklin has never made a production out of acknowledging his peers or superiors in the NFL, but Lombardi he respects, sometimes with a snarl and sometimes with a wisecrack. Sunday he did it with absolute humility.

"We beat," he told Lombardi, "the best."

"Your team played well," Lombardi said. "It's a credit to you, coach."

Van Brocklin would have given five grand for that on the market.

"Vince Lombardi," he told a pal, "has got class."

But downtown in Green Bay, they weren't so sure about the Packers.

In Green Bay, young couples don't whisper sweet endearments over candlelit dinners.

"Honey," a half-oiled brunette asked her date in the Tuxedo Bar, "what happened to the Packers?"

The guy said, "Sweetie, we just weren't getting that rush on Tarkenton. Now you got to give the Vikings credit. They're tough. I think they ought to become one of our traditional rivals."

"But we've only been playing the Vikings for six years," she said softly.

"Honey," the guy said, "the way Tarkenton does it to us, it's traditional."

I wandered into a downtown supper club and asked a waitress for directions. She was carrying a tray and tried to dodge. I dodged, too, but the wrong way and we bumped.

"How do you like that?" she said. "In Minneapolis, even the mashers scramble."

A Village Buries Its Soldier

HANSKA, Minnesota – The rice paddies of Viet Nam are half a world from the untroubled high cornfields of a southern Minnesota village called Hanska – and the hilltop cemetery where Corporal Denny Wellmann was buried Sunday.

They will never be so distant to this community again.

Dirt farmers with big, reddened hands and bowed shoulders wept Sunday before the sealed, flag-covered coffin in the lovely white Unitarian church where the 21-year-old Marine had worshipped as a boy.

Mourners filled the tiny church and the adjacent service rooms, and when there were no seats left there, they gathered in the churchyard.

To most of them, townspeople and neighboring farm families, he had been more than just another boy in the community; a laughing, fun-craving kid who lit their affections whether he was trying to be a farmer or a salesman at the Green Clothiers in New Ulm.

He lived in a world of sunshine, bowling parties, baseball and auto drives.

And now he was lying dead in their church, a little more than one month after writing to his father:

"We took a lot of casualties again (in our last battle). Just thank God that the dear Lord is looking after me. I think, daddy, I am going to cry when I get home, I am going to be so happy."

He had been a good Marine, promoted in recent months to lance corporal, and, although he had confided to a friend in a letter that "I just hope we are fighting for something worthwhile," his letters home rarely bore a trace of self-sympathy or resentment.

He had fought in many of the major engagements through the long, broiling spring and summer in Viet Nam, once being wounded in the arm by shrapnel.

A week ago two Marine officers appeared at the home of his sister, Mrs. Roger Breu of Searles, Minnesota, with the news that her brother had been killed at Quang Tri by fragments of an explosive device.

To spare his ailing father the initial shock, he had asked the Marines to inform his sister first in the event of his death.

His father, Elmer Wellmann, 60, had understood that.

"Denny was that way," Elmer Wellmann said Sunday morning in the family kitchen. He wore overalls, and there was grime on his still-powerful hands. He had been in the farmyard most of the morning, assisting his other sons and son-in-law with chores.

"I had some bad heart trouble a while back," Wellmann said. "Denny kept writing me to stay away from the work, that his brothers would take care of the farm."

"That war is so far away," he said. "It's just so hard to understand. But I think it is right that we are there. I would never want to believe that we lost our boy in a useless war.

"My four other boys all were in the service, and they came back. I made myself believe that Denny would come back the same way. But I guess none of us knows what it is really like in Viet Nam."

The little town near where the Wellmanns live is the essence of the rural Midwest, a Scandinavian village of 500 with simple, neat frame homes, a handful of stores, a couple of taverns, a bowling alley.

The war in Viet Nam had been remote and bewildering to its townspeople, less so for the Wellmanns and the parents of Tommy Helling and Darrel Asleson, two other Hanska servicemen who are in Viet Nam today.

They had expected personal tragedy here in World War II, when the war was intimate to everyone and when the goals and purposes seemed clear and explicit.

But with Viet Nam the sense of personal involvement was not so close, and the horror of men dying was further removed.

Until Sunday.

The Reverend Emil Gudmundson of Des Moines, Iowa, until two years ago the Wellmanns' pastor in Hanska, understood this and spoke of it in his eulogy of the boy of whom he had been so fond.

"There was a time," he said, "when the warrior was a hero — his sacrifice exemplary. But in today's world, war is neither simple nor an upsurge of value and sacrifice.

"There is a confusion of purposes: Among them a struggle for liberation and freedom and a striving against oppression on the one hand; and a bestiality on the other with the ever-present threat that the utilization of our grisly technology may destroy our values and our way of life, and even our lives, in perhaps half an hour."

How then, he asked, do you memorialize a Minnesota farm boy who gave his life in a war he may not have understood?

"Let us be neither bitter nor vindictive," he said, "to any who are caught up in the violence of today, for such makes mockery of our greatest hopes and beliefs.

"Let us instead focus on the single individual life we knew as Dennis Wellmann. We recall the young man with the winning smile, the disarming personality, the easy conversationalist, the apparently carefree outlook."

But his letters from Viet Nam, the clergyman continued, had revealed a greater depth to the young man, "with the direction of his values, his ambitions and his potential beginning to come clear."

And yet it was hard to identify death, the minister said, "with a person who so loved life." This was the breezy and popular high school student at New Ulm, the smiling salesman at Green Clothiers, the boy who had won awards for FFA and 4-H work— although he was never quite sure, until he had been exposed to mortar and machine gun fire in Viet Nam, that he was going to be a farmer for the rest of his life.

He had written to two of his friends in New Ulm, Carl (Red) Wyczawski and school-teacher John Oien:

"I just hope I don't change too much by the time I come home. I don't want to get like some men do from war. The only thing I can say is I am going to do everything in my power not to change."

Sunday on the hilltop cemetery a Marine honor guard folded the flag above his casket in the light breeze of a radiant September day.

A Marine sergeant took the flag and tenderly placed it in the hands of Dennis Wellmann's mother.

He saluted.

Tune in for the Latest Calamities

I have never been as relieved to see a snowstorm in all my life.

This is not one of those cases of narrow selfishness. Personally, I hold the view that you see one blizzard and you have pretty well seen them all, and that on the Iron Range years ago today's blizzard would have been mild enough to mark the opening day of the spring thaw.

But no, I was thinking about the professional reputations of some of my pals at WCCO radio, the only station in town which not only forecasts and reports the weather but psychoanalyzes it — sharing its little triumphs, interpreting its moods and apologizing for its delinquencies.

I was drawn to the station shortly after 1:30 p.m. Tuesday when an acquaintance confided downtown, "Well, they are forecasting a blizzard for Breckenridge."

"Not," I responded, "again."

It was such an unnaturally balmy day, so temperate and tame that the very slush in the curbs seemed mellow and sociable, a sloppy old friend adrip with the promise of spring.

Confidently, I flipped on the car radio and monitored Charlie Boone in the afternoon. Boone happens to be one of my favorite professionals, a well-sheened and effortless craftsman in whom I have come to place absolute trust despite his occasional breathless infatuation with the weather.

Charlie is talking about plunging temperatures and winds gusting up to 40 miles per hour in Grand Forks, N. D. The stuff is heading across the Northwest, Charlie says, and may be in the Twin Cities area by early evening. Dick Chapman interrupts to impart scope to the news by contrasting the Dakota blizzard to 74 degree temperatures in Dodge City, Kansas.

"You can't afford not to listen to WCCO," I am advised.

Shaken, I return to the office to perform the ritual prescribed whenever the station tells me a blizzard is coming. Wordlessly I strap on my Korean military boots, sprinkle sand in them and pinch my nose several times so as to redden it and make it more discernible to oncoming pedestrians. I walk into the street carrying the status symbols of the downtown businessman, a shovel and a pail of ashes.

I return to Charlie on my car radio.

"Now it may be beautiful where you are," Charlie observes, "but it's getting kind of tough . . . . Well, winter is coming back . . . it's moving toward us . . . that weatherball is flickering white."

Charlie sighs. His problem is that the station is an electronic octopus that spreads itself all over the territory. What one suction cup feels in South Dakota may not be what another feels in Wisconsin. What this means is that Boone has to be light on his suction cups, and that while he is telling one tentacle to come in out of the seaweed, he is telling another it's all right to squirm around in the sargasso.

This is described in the trade as public service, and quite seriously I would like to note that nobody in the country surpasses WCCO at it. Boone now leaves to be succeeded by teams of oracles, AAA reporters, stuttering weather balls, twin clocks and men in towers.

Howard Viken views the oncoming calamity with restraint, however, because the snow still hasn't arrived as advertised. At 7:20, my friend Sid comes on with Johnny Kundla in the basketball preview. Sid has run through the list of candidates for the Viking coaching job and has now exchanged his tea leaves for a stethoscope, with which he is diagnosing Kundla's ulcers again.

I begin now, however, to sense some alarm in the station's weather reports. An announcer at half-time makes no mention of blizzards but refers to a simple cold wave warning. He is back at 9:15 p.m., still without the advertised precipitation and acknowledges that "there are no snow reports tonight from any of our reporting stations in Minnesota."

But he says it with a stubborn faith, like H. V. Kaltenborn waiting for the rural precincts to come in. I switch to Rodger Kent's weather on TV channel 11 and come totally unglued by this slap-happy style of soothsaying and cannot comprehend the weather at all at this point. Back on WCCO radio, Chapman acknowledges that the weather tonight is "changeable." Where IS the snow?

But I look out a window at 11 p.m. and it is snowing. I get up at 5 a.m. It is still snowing. Boone is vindicated. Chapman is vindicated. I am vindicated. It is snowing, and I am glad. Glad. Glad.

Indomitable Ben the Duffer

The spectacle of calm and unhurried ineptness has always intrigued me.

I think it takes no particular character, for example, to be a bad golfer and to fill the fairways with wails and miserable apologies with each shanked drive and flubbed putt.

Bad golfers of this genre bore me. On the other hand, you have a man like Ben Berger who plays bad golf with a great and majestic serenity, oblivious to the mounting strokes and the snickers of lower mortals around him.

Berger has been hacking at golf courses for 35 years, a span in which his radiant incompetence has come to be recognized by eminent authorities from Oak Ridge to Miami Beach.

Thirty-five years admittedly is a long time to be playing golf without breaking 100. Berger has managed it with imperturbable ease. Friends regard him as the only golfer in town who has never experienced a serious slump.

He has been known, however, to produce strange twitches and traumatic after-effects among some of the game's most distinguished players who have been thrown into combat with him.

Sam Snead, for example, to this day refuses to play another round at Oak Ridge, where he came totally unhinged 15 years ago on the first hole of a pro-am tournament in which Benny was his partner.

Berger stepped to the tee, waggled pudgily and swung. As Snead watched aghast, the ball sputtered 10 feet BEHIND the tee, describing a flopping parabola before hitting a tree and expiring at the feet of Snead's caddie.

"Surely this has got to be a jest," Snead observed. "Either that or this man is one of the best trick shots I have ever seen."

"No," an Oak Ridge regular explained. "That ball didn't carry too badly for one of Benny's tee shots, although I'll admit the direction was a little off."

Clearly shaken, Snead pounded his tee shot into a lake.

He never did recover. Golf historians have recorded, as a matter of fact, that Snead's nerves were so frazzled by the experience of a round with Berger as to leave him with a case of lingering yips for months. It got so bad that Snead was finishing out of the money in some of the later tournaments that year.

And so I found the prospect of a round with Benny irresistible. Readers may recall that my own game vacillates between being routinely bad and inventively atrocious.

We convened at Oak Ridge a couple of days ago, Benny, the White House's Irv Schectman and sportscaster Paul Giel, who showed up with a snappy sweater and an atomizer.

I was intercepted at the clubhouse by Midge Berger, the theater man's wife and golfing adviser.

"You have been recommended," she said amiably, "as one of the few men in town who is capable of losing to my husband. My only advice is not to tense up."

Berger shook my hand with that unruffleable sweet calm, and I knew it was going to be a struggle. Giel and Schectman whacked their drives down the fairway. Benny addressed his ball with a style which I can only describe as early period submariner. He zipped his drive 30 yards through the tee box, the ball doglegging slightly after striking a twig.

Benny smiled. "I haven't been playing much this year," he confided. "But it wasn't bad, everything considered. I'll take it."

I, of course, sliced my drive miserably, over the trees and out of bounds.

"You're being psyched like Snead," Schectman said sternly. "Take hold of yourself, man."

Grimly, I pulled myself together and salvaged an eight on the hole. But I had to keep looking over my shoulder, because Berger was applying stubborn pressure all the way, eating up that fairway at 30 yards a stroke.

He got down in nine, and I rubbed the perspiration from my forehead.

"I would have been all right," he said, "but I scuffed my fifth shot. Looks like a great day for golf."

Well, it was. I have to tell you in all honesty that I did not lose to Berger's eventual 136, but it was a near thing. Not even Giel survived unscathed. On the 12th he punched two out of bounds and one over the green for a 10.

Berger whipped him with an indomitable nine.

A Greenhorn Solos at the Opera

Before launching the diet which no doubt permanently and immortally altered his physique, the writer attempted one final fling as a fat man by undertaking the ambition of a lifetime — an appearance with the Metropolitan Opera Company.

Seven safety pins stood between the Metropolitan Opera company and disaster at Northrop Auditorium Wednesday night.

The hero of the evening was not Sandor Konya, the passionate tenor who sang Rudolfo in Jock Puccini's "La Boheme" but rather a costume manager who fashioned a chain of pins to hold up my trousers.

As a result, my debut with the Met — while it may have escaped the attention of some of the more superficial critics — was an undiluted success.

I was summoned by the university's chief of supernumeraries last week to play the role of a French soldier in the opera's second act. The only instructions were to bring your own black shoes and socks. The job specifications called for 20 seconds on stage.

With rare devotion, however, I spent the better part of the week honing up on the intricacies of the plot and marching in front of my record player.

The reason for this was that only once or twice in a man's career is he confronted with that priceless opportunity wherein his own talents blend perfectly with the demands of the part.

I should add that there was one other instruction — "under no conditions will you sing or open your mouth in any way as though threatening to sing."

This was a mild put-down, but one accepts such inhibitions for the sake of his art.

With 11 other supers, I showed up at 7 p.m. with black shoes and socks. A stage manager, Stanley Levine, viewed me warily.

"Our request was for thin, gaunt-type people to play the soldiers," Levine said. "You look overfed. We have no openings for mess sergeants in the soldier scene."

"All I ask," I said, stricken, "is a trial. You won't regret it."

Levine wavered. The man had heart, all right, and the costume manager had a string of safety pins.

They handed me a pair of scarlet trousers with a 30-inch waist. I slipped my right leg through but got no more than thigh-high with the left one. There was a zipper there but I couldn't negotiate the first link. The problem: To secure the waist flaps without exposing my polka-dot shorts.

"You look like a seven-pin man," the costume expert said professionally.

"Is that a record?" I asked.

"No, but it will keep you out of jail."

By now the fashionable first-night crowd was surging into the auditorium, unaware of the drama being played out in the catacombs below.

Somebody gave me a blue cape and a plumed shako. Leaning against a tuba, I lit a cigarette in a show of elaborate nonchalance, but I must tell you I was aflutter inside.

At this moment one of the pins unfastened and stabbed me in the hip. I could have complained, I suppose, but there is an old tradition about these things.

I walked backstage and observed soprano Lucine Amara, serene and unruffled, adjusting her prop-candle in its tray. I knew then the company was going to carry the evening once more.

Heidi Krall swung into Musetta's Waltz in the second act and we lined up two abreast for our entry. The costume man was there faithfully at my side, checking my pins.

The band moved out and there we were striding across the stage as 4,800 people looked on worshipfully. It was a moment of a lifetime. The pins held, as I knew they would.

But it was all over much too quickly. And now the curtain came closed, and the crowd was yelling, "bravo, bravo."

Oh, I know it was an hallucination born of the headiness of the moment, but I could have sworn some of them were yelling, "soldiers, soldiers."

Later, Levine passed out dollar bills to each of the soldiers. "Another day," I said coolly, "another dollar."

The Princesses of Picadilly

PICADILLY CIRCUS, LONDON – With a sense of sadness I have to inform you that the miniskirt has succeeded where the German Luftwaffe failed and has left London exposed and quivering, a sitting target for the next fashion house con game.

As a part of a serious piece of clinical work, I have viewed a thousand promenading knees on London's Broadway during the past three hours and have reached this tentative conclusion:

Never in the field of human endeavor has so little fabric been lifted so high to reveal so much that needed to be concealed so badly.

No man in his rational mind is going to object to a moderate dose of the thigh-high exhibitionism which succeeded the Beatles as England's most recent contribution to world culture.

The trouble with the miniskirt is that – like any painting or length of sausage – it has to be hung from the right frame for maximum effectiveness.

As five million GIs will assure you, there is nothing wrong with London women. And purely from casual observation I would guess the incidence of knobby knees, bow legs and wobbly calves is no higher in England than in the United States, Italy, Germany, and Switzerland, and probably lower than in Liechtenstein.

I did not visit France, on the theory that it disturbs one's timetables to have to genuflect at the borders in order not to violate the country's historical sanctity and exclusivity. Besides this, De Gaulle was busy in conference with St. Michael the Archangel.

But in England, the miniskirt fetish has spread beyond all reasonable bounds. They wear miniskirts on the streets, in the Tube, in schools, at cricket matches, in the Tower of London and, for all I know, in Winchester Cathedral.

Conservatively, I'd guess the garment is misplaced on about 80 per cent of the exhibitors. London, of course, has stamina and can take it. I don't have that kind of endurance and therefore approached one of the flimsy-skirted practitioners for some advice on how long the freak show would last.

My informant was a Miss Valerie Mitchell, 22, a London club singer who was wearing a fringed black miniskirt that expired a foot above the knee.

"Have you ever been mistaken," I asked tactfully, "for a delinquent?"

"The style here is regarded as smart, modern, and rather dramatic," she said. "Yes, there is a good deal of exhibitionism involved, but there is nothing wrong with attracting the attention of the other sex, is there?"

"There are girls who should wear them, I suppose, and those who shouldn't," I replied cautiously. "On you the effect is so stunning and provocative as to be almost illegal. On the other hand, I saw miniskirts on at least three pregnant women in West Berlin, and concluded there ought to be some kind of international law about now."

In view of the galloping trend toward miniskirts in Britain and elsewhere, I asked Miss Mitchell for the smart European woman's impression of fashion tastes among American women — who, I explained, have not yet plowed full throttle into the miniskirt area.

"American women," Miss Mitchell said with some brittleness, "are improving in their tastes."

"But they still lag behind Europeans?" I asked.

"It is a matter of geography, perhaps," Miss Mitchell said tolerantly. "American women do seem to be a bit more conservative than women here but are, as I said, getting along better now."

Did Miss Mitchell believe there would be some sort of high hemline retreat soon?

"My goodness, it has cost a good deal of money for British women to convert to miniskirts. We couldn't afford to go back to conventional lengths now, could we?"

"How do you suppose," I asked, "the fashion people make money? We have the same situation in America, only we do it with automobiles."

Miss Mitchell was smoothly contoured, chic and generously endowed, all of which seemed rather incongruous with the dirigible-shaped pork sausage she was consuming at the buffet counter of the downtown pub.

"I notice," I observed, "you do not seem overly concerned about calories. This is the place where the child phenomenon, Twiggy, burst upon world fashion. Don't most of London's young women try to duplicate Twiggy's straight and level geometry?"

"Twiggy," my informant declared, "is too skinny. Most of the women in London will agree with that. She does have this type of gimmick working for her, of course, but I'm sure she created a far greater stir in America than she has in England."

"How would you explain that?"

"Surely you must know more about American psychology and salesmanship than I do. I'm sure I do not know what is exportable about Twiggy."

This put us generally in the same camp because I never really understood what was importable about Twiggy, let alone exportable.

Miss Mitchell stylishly disposed of the last bite of her sausage, quaffed the final draft of her Guinness beer and neatly slipped her mini-raincoat over her miniskirt.

"It is gratifying," I advised myself, "to be physically present here at the very seat of high fashion and taste."

And yet, still unsure about the implications for American society, I interrogated a 20-year-old receptionist at the Pan-American booking office a few blocks down Picadilly.

"I think it's a little silly for most girls to be wearing the real mini-mini-skirts," Miss Carol Boldt observed, "but I don't think the hemline will ever go back down below the knee. And you would be amazed by the effect this is having on American tourists.

"The girls come to Europe wearing the longer American skirts. When they go back to America they're wearing mini-skirts even shorter than the ones we're wearing."

"Do you think the far-out trend will reach as far as Minneapolis?" I asked.

"Where?"

"Minneapolis. It's in what you would call the Midlands of America."

"Why not?" she replied sweetly. "In this day and age, all things are possible."

Van and Fran Depart, Separately and Equally

At the very worst, you will have to credit the Vikings with a novel solution to the problem of a feuding coach and quarterback.

True, they did manage to lose both of them. In the process, the Vikings relieved themselves of a million dollars worth of talent and the two personalities on the club who made it marketable from coast-to-coast and acceptable to CBS program directors.

Vikings fans may console themselves with the knowledge, however, that the resignations of Norm Van Brocklin and Fran Tarkenton finally restored control of the club to the owners. I'm not sure this is a plus. In any event, it lays the groundwork for an exciting new five-year plan, our third.

Nobody can reasonably fault the club owners, of course, for the mutual decision of Van Brocklin and Tarkenton to seek separate maintenance. With the Vikings, resignations have become a fad approaching the snowmobile craze and have left General Manager Jim Finks as the only office supervisor in the city who now makes a nose count after the morning coffee break.

As far as I know, there were no new resignations today, but it is early. You will note, however, that the list of fugitives does not include the club treasurer, who is still counting 1966 profits approaching seven figures – and who will be counting the same kind of figures 12 months from now when all the calamities are forgotten.

The one disappointment in the aftermath is the fresh attempt by well-intentioned but somewhat forgetful people to confer sainthood on Van Brocklin, who does not need it.

I don't mind the attempted canonization of the Dutchman as much as the parallel indictment of Tarkenton as some kind of agitator who broke up the team in a willful and self-serving campaign for money and glorification.

My first reaction to this is to note that no game played with an inflated bladder is worth all that vehemence. My second is to say to the prosecutors, "Ah, come off of it."

The Dutchman is at his best in the free-swinging, needle-flinging, roistering society of the football man when he does not have to worry about images, cues, counter-attractions or rewriting club history.

He hacked his way through pro football's jungle to become a great player on nerve, intelligence and ability. He was, and is, a first-rate football coach. But when he is grieving about Tarkenton's lively devotion to personal interests, he must be forgetting about his own such devotion in Los Angeles ten years ago.

The things friends and associates have found so admirable in Van Brocklin socially are his spontaneity, a total lack of pretension and a natural impulse to talk off the top of his cap, irreverently and sometimes outrageously. It follows that what Dutch regards as absolute honesty and frankness, in his own mind, does not always represent the objective truth.

So long as he commanded the gut loyalties of his ballplayers and made them better men with his fury and his nose-thumbing at the odds, Van Brocklin was a great leader. Something went out of them and him when he stepped out for a day two years ago. They believed him less, followed him less ardently.

He is the last man in football I would consider a competitive quitter. But for all of the mental toughness in him there is also much of the little boy, who likes to be liked. When his furies spilled over and offended and alienated people who were once his friends — such as players and coaches — it seemed to him a repudiation of his values and a humiliation to his pride.

Nobody pushed Dutch into resigning — the owners, fans, writers, players. Especially Tarkenton did not push him, and any suggestion that he did is simply a falsification of the record.

There is in the makeup of a man like this, who is maddening at times and impossible at others but so admirable in many other ways, a capacity for self-injury, most easily understood by those who have the same capacity.

It is a regret to see him go but equally a regret to see Tarkenton go. You would have thought the two of them could have found some grounds for accommodation — such as money.

The Dutchman? Well, you just know that he can sit around for a year and watch the coaching offers flood in when other coaches start resigning or are pushed.

Tarkenton?

Do not worry about Tarkenton.

Eight-Cylinder Emerald from Detroit

In the spirit of sweet charity and forbearance, I forgave Detroit for all of its iniquities last week and bought a new car.

It was not a decision to which I gave long and prayerful deliberation. If I had, I would have talked myself out of it. I don't have that much faith in Detroit. The simple truth is that my old car was about to expire and was, in fact, in an advanced stage of delirium tremens when I coddled it the last mile into a car dealer's garage.

The people there pawed my old car like understanding morticians. It wasn't one of THEIR creatures, so they didn't have to apologize.

The car I owned was not intended, either by ancestry or design, to run more than a couple of years without a major transfusion and it had gotten about as much blood out of me as it was entitled to.

Affectionately, I gave the rear bumper one final tap of my shoe for auld lang syne, and the thing nearly collapsed. With cool and sympathetic professionalism, a salesman moved in on me with a sales form, a pen and an ignition key.

I didn't sign without a few flickering reservations. As a rule, people around you interpret the sight of a new automobile as the mark of some sudden and undeserved opulence, and betray in their eyes the hovering suspicion that you must have knocked off a bank or drugged your aunt.

Nevertheless, I was willing to endure all of that to spare my employers the embarrassment of building a hitch-hike station outside the front entrance.

I was awash in these thoughts of self-sacrifice when they wheeled before me my new automobile, glistening, virginal and freshly endorsed by the finance company.

Well, it was gorgeous, purely, candidly and turquoisely. It held me bewitched and humble, ashamed of my doubts about Detroit and grateful for the gum wrappers I had saved as a child to deserve such bounty.

You are entitled, I think, to share the first-day chronicle of a life rekindled and a flagging faith restored by this miracle of free enterprise.

3:30 p.m. — I seat myself in the new car and inhale. Alongside the vinyl perfume of a new automobile, lilacs in the spring, and new-mown hay are stale and malodorous. The salesman is looking in through the front door window with an apostolic smile and his eyes are saying, "You've waited a long time for this baby and in just two years it'll be all yours."

3:32 p.m. — I turn the ignition key and the car won't start.

Horrified, I look at the salesman but he is imperturbable. "The automatic shift," he says. "You've got it set in reverse."

3:35 p.m. — I am out on the street and I tell you I have never seen such wild, undisciplined drivers. I maneuver to stay away from them because, brother, if anyone is going to hit this car he is going to be served with a Supreme Court injunction, a habeas corpus and a delinquent garbage bill, and I will see to that personally.

4 p.m. — Passersby begin to notice my new car, as I secretly hoped they would. I nod at them with patrician reserve. A generously stacked blonde at a downtown intersection purrs through an open window: "Are you heading south?"

"Sorry, honey," I say with dignity, "another time."

4:30 p.m. — I am loose on the open highway, driving in a rhapsody of silence. I feel like doing figure eights. As a matter of fact, I DO figure eights but am induced to change my geometry by the sight of a squad car.

9:30 a.m. — I emerge from the office to find a parking ticket stuck into the hidden windshield wiper, an act which required a high degree of exploratory skill on the part of the patrolman. It strikes me as a desecration, but I pay. They have nicked me so often now that the boys have set up a drive-in window at City Hall.

10:30 a.m. — I detect the first flakes of fallen dust on the hood, and I am morose. The car suddenly seems depressingly old.

11:30 a.m. —I drive back to the garage. The serviceman appears surprised.

"A 50-mile checkup?" he asks. "No, we usually request a little more distance than that. Why don't you ride around the block a couple of times?"

You see how it is. It doesn't take long for reality to catch up with you.

'I Didn't Know the Stein Was Loaded'

MUNICH, West Germany — I made the mistake of ordering a glass of beer in Munich last night.

I didn't know the stein was loaded, or that I was embarking on a gastronomic nightmare that would undo six months of dieting and leave me pining for the easy calm of polka night and Chinese New Year at Mayslack's Bar.

You say your neighborhood pub was a little congested and boisterous over the weekend, somebody blew foam on your lapels and they ran out of pitchers?

Will you imagine a tavern seating 7,000 people?

And all of them singing maniacally sentimental songs in beery harmony, for five hours at a sitting?

And there are four bands working in relays, with four tuba players in reserve in case the musicians join the crowd and forget about playing?

And sometimes the service is a trifle slow because the waitresses are thinking ahead of the musicians and have already joined the crowd themselves?

And that if you are a beer-drinker or tavern-crawler you have not had this kind of hysterically good time in all your life?

Friends, there are not only one but two joints in town answering the description and I'm sure there are a dozen more except that I got caught at a table where they link arms and lurch rhythmically, at times in unison, and bellow "ein prosit" all night.

Don't misunderstand. I was in no hurry to leave. It would have been irrelevant even if I were. Munichers are the only people in the world required by the city charter to have fun and raise hell. They pursue this civic obligation devoutly, single-mindedly, and aggressively.

The chief rivals in the stein-pushing competition here are the universally-advertised Hofbrauhaus and an even bigger beer and bratwurst arena called the Mathaser.

There are times when the places get so jammed the owners have seriously considered selling season tickets.

And yet I found the more famous Hofbrauhaus tame alongside the uproarious gemutlichkeit of the Mathaser, which claims to sell something like 55,000 liters of beer (approximately quarts) a week — golden, flowing Lowenbrau, the beer that has been fermenting for more than 600 years.

I entered through the main vestibule, past a diner who was drinking his soup standing up, not from a plate or a bowl but from a full-size tureen. The vestibule was aswarm with beer-drinkers, pretzel stands and charging waiters.

I walked into a restaurant, made my way through another, then another. I am asking you to believe 15 restaurants in one tavern, and a movie theater for diversion!

You have to walk through arcaded terraces and beer gardens, muraled keg rooms, tipsy customers. When they go to the tavern in Munich everybody goes with them – their baby sitters, their creditors and their pitch pipes.

I was lost in a jungle of bratwurst somewhere near the basement dining rooms and started making my way upstairs.

"Where," I demanded of the nearest waiter, "can I get a beer?"

He led me to one of the active restaurants and opened the door. A landslide of sound jarred me.

Most of it came from the bandstand. There were 10 musicians with lederhosen, knobby knees, and instruments. Their leader was a rollicking fat man with a girth of heroic dimensions. It heaved in sections, in harmony with the beat, and he kept drinking beer between licks on the trombone.

The boys were in form and a thousand voices refrained "Nach Hause" and all the other beer hall masterworks, and the waiter was coming at me with one of those one-liter flagons of beer, about a quart of Lowenbrau costing the equivalent of 37 cents.

"How much does it cost at the Hofbrauhaus?" I asked one of my tablemates, a mediocre baritone from East Munich.

"It is a mark and 50 pfennigs here, but only a mark and 35 pfennigs at the Hofbrauhaus. There, however, you get more foam."

A waiter challenged him. "They have the same price," he argued, "but you are right, they have more foam." A Hofbrauhaus loyalist challenged both of them. They were coming now with the pretzels, huge, labyrinthal pretzels the size of horseshoes.

I asked one of the waitresses, a saucy, middle-aged Bavarian, where the beer came from, meaning where was it made. This she interpreted as a reflection on the beer's freshness, and she reacted violently.

Nobody stands on ceremony in the beer halls. Seizing my hand, the waitress ran me down three flights of steps to the kegs from which the amber was flowing. Direct from the pump.

"How," I asked the waiter, returning, "do you compare American beer with Munich beer?"

The waiter smiled sympathetically. "Mein lieber freund," he said, "when you go to Paris you do not order hamburger."

Although canted somewhat to the left by now, I headed for the Hofbrauhaus, dodging the mini-skirted belles of the avenue and the discotheque joints across the street, where they prefer rock to rostbraten.

Maybe it was the hour, but I found the Haufbrauhaus relatively dull alongside the Mathaser until somebody at a table of ten across the aisle decided to cheer this nomadic American. There were now three liters of beer in front of me. I passed up two of them with thanks and convivial sign language. Misunderstanding, they tried to be amicable next with glasses of schnapps.

I surrendered and joined the party. Somebody was bringing in a plate of wiener schnitzel with potato salad and green salad and goulash soup and rolls, and somebody wanted me to sample the bratwurst. And the eight trombone and tuba players were playing "ein prosit" again . . .

This is all being confessed to you this morning over a small plate of Melba toast especially ordered from the nearest lebensmittel.

I have an appointment with a guy from the Mathaser who tells me, "Now if you really want to taste the greatest beer made, it's Edelstoff at the Augstiner."

I am not going to pronounce it, much less drink it.

Rebellion of the Coffee Machine

No doubt we all admire the audacity and vision of the button-pushers who want to build a machine-tooled experimental city in which nobody will have troubles.

The idea outlined this week by Athelstan Spilhaus is so good it ought to be spared the obvious teasing. My only reservation is that we should proceed slowly on this and ask ourselves the question:

Are we truly in such a galloping hurry to enter a society in which the psychiatrists will be out of work because there are no neurotics; dry cleaners will be eliminated because motorists will have no puddles to charge through in the hope of wrecking pedestrians' clothes; and life will be so blissful as to make judges, cops, and insurance companies obsolete?

It must be clear to you that we cannot afford all of this unemployment at the moment and, beyond this, do we really want to entrust a computerized future to the same people who make coffee vending machines?

The question is raised in view of the recent eccentric performance of the office coffee machine. Like you, I have been struck by the close parallel between the behavior of human beings under duress and the conduct of the typical coffee machine.

Being compassionate, I have excused the actions of our dispenser on the theory that any machine is entitled to a swollen spigot now and then or a form of cogwheel hangover. But this machine undeniably needs professional help.

This I sought from the sales manager of the ARA company, which operates some 1,500 mechanical peddlers in the Twin Cities.

"Is there a hospital," I asked Fred (Lefty) Luedke, "for sick machines?"

"There is no such thing," Luedke replied stoutly, "as a bad machine. Bad coins, bad mechanics and impatient coffee-drinkers, yes. But if you're asking are there such things as machines that are incorrigible – that is, impervious to treatment and sympathetic handling – I say no. Any machine, if it has the right kind of character and deep down has its wiring in the right place, can be reformed."

And yet this did not altogether reassure me. I recalled a

society editor around here who was accosted on her hands and knees in front of the machine one day, desperately filling coffee cups.

There were 15 cups standing around her, brimful, and she was howling for help. "The machine won't stop pouring coffee," she wailed.

All the while the machine's innards kept grinding ominously, as though the creature were in the midst of some great gastronomic rebellion.

"Yes," Luedke said clinically, "it was the solenoid, which controls the machine's nervous system. Coffee machines, as you know, are very much like people. They are subject to fatigue and, in circumstances of stress, to a type of shell shock. I would say the machine's chief hazards are a defective solenoid and a kick in the dispenser.

"Now you think that lady might have had troubles. We had a case years ago of a J. C. Penney store in which a machine was hooked up to the city water. This may have been before there were safety devices. Anyhow, the machine didn't cut out when everybody went home for the weekend. When the manager got there on Monday, the joint was up to the ceiling in coffee. When we got there with help we found him pulling his hair with one hand and pushing a squeegee with the other.

"Another time, trying to sell one of our machines to a gas station manager, we installed the machine, dropped in a coin and handed him a cup of flavorful coffee. He put the cup to his lips and the bottom fell out, flooding his vest with hot coffee.

"Now, I have seen angry coffee drinkers kick, maim, slug and curse the machine. I have seen a man wind up from 20 feet away and fling himself at the machine, and all he got for his violence was lumpy cream. I mean you have to have some tolerance. We make 25 to 30 service calls a day. It isn't as though those machines are cold, calculating human beings.

"They tell me of a case where some infuriated foundry workers took a fork lift, wheeled it under a coffee machine and dumped it – without waiting for change – into a kiln of molten metal."

The machine came to an ironic end, melted down to make a case of dripless percolators—destined to dispense coffee forever without getting another dime.

How to Receive Indecent Proposals

Friends have looked on in transfixed horror while I have systematically converted myself from a blimpy eyesore into a hard-muscled Adonis.

I am aware that I have flouted destiny in some small measure and retain a nagging sense of having tampered with the laws of nature. It wasn't intended that I should become a cool, reckless, handsome devil in mid-career, but there it is, and I am powerless to change the chemistry now.

All of this is not without its penalties. While it is true I have shed 31 pounds in 5½ weeks, can now leap tall divans with one vault, and can beat the self-propelled traffic cop to my parking meter, there are embarrassing trappings to this second life.

It is awkward, for example, to receive indecent proposals from strange women on the telephone in the middle of the afternoon.

I simply do not have time to handle all of these impedimenta, and the worst part of it is that I see no immediate end to my predicament.

You have undoubtedly guessed what has happened. I began dieting and toning up a little more than a month ago and now have what the coaches describe as momentum. I cannot turn it off.

You say you want some of the action?

I am going to tell you how you can get it, but I want no dialogue on the subject, no mail from scoffers or cream-hearted bleaters, no rebuttal from sore-headed temporizers who can't stand the pressures and no calls from pill-pushers and diet arbiters.

I adhere to the philosophy, also subscribed to by the Dodge rebellion advertisers and coaches who use the first team for 3½ quarters while winning 49-0, that nothing succeeds like excess.

Granted, there is nothing more noxious than a reformed reprobate. It is a matter of record, however, that I used to average four manhattans, a beer, three packs of cigarettes and 2,800 calories a day, with sleepless nights and, if you must know, nagging backache.

If you are anywhere close to being thus categorized, I want

you to stop smoking — now. Stop boozing, and content yourself with one fix of bourbon a day with three bottles of low-calorie cola for a chase. For breakfast take juice and grapefruit, for lunch consomme and cottage cheese, for dinner, steak, lettuce salad, nonfat milk or tea and large amounts of self-righteousness. No pills, drugs, or injections.

Exercise. Join the "Y," some health club, or the highwaymen down the street. It doesn't impress me that doctors, authors, and other velvet-glovers tell you not to give up everything at once.

As for the other dimension to this, I have conducted an informal poll and get mixed reaction on the sexual effects among truly dedicated spartans. The only recommendation to adults here is that if you have a normal sex life, regard yourself as fortunate. If you have no sex life, write a book. If you have an abnormal sex life write General Mills for a Wheaties supplement.

Now in the event you are hesitating, I should tell you that inside of two weeks my doctor was getting curious, inside of three weeks he was calling me for an appointment and inside of four he had joined the "Y."

Oh, there are temptations, but if he is haughty and smug enough, a man can override those. Under certain conditions, it is even possible for a woman to do it. In this connection, I like the suggestion of a sporting type named Sid Hartman, who quite improbably comes forward as a campaigner for Save-the-Stout-Ladies.

Hartman suggests dietetic restaurants, even co-educational dietetic restaurants, where we may all of us commune over platters of carrot sticks and unsalted radishes.

As a matter of fact, he put to me the startling proposal last week that delicatessens may be overlooking something good by not investigating the market for dietetic bagels.

But you see how a man can become evangelistic on the subject. I established a team record in Ann Arbor last week by keeping Hartman away from the telephones for 45 seconds of uninterrupted conversation.

Now I ask you, if anything is that compelling, can it be all bad?

While you are deliberating, please pass the jug of Tab.

The Lonely Genius of Mousey's Bar

The world's greatest genius viewed me tolerantly. He sat in one of the beer-marinated back booths of Mousey's Bar on 12th and Hennepin, the throbbing epicenter of the city's culture cauldron.

"I never realized at what point I became an all-around genius," explained Raymond De Gagnon. "People who know me were content to call me the greatest dancer of all time, and let it go at that.

"Actually, this understates the case and does me an injustice. My other works have now advanced to the extent that I'm afraid only Albert Einstein could understand them.

"Unfortunately, he died."

Silently we mourned the passing of the great mathematician, mutually regretting that he should have gone before accepting the ultimate challenge of a lifetime of achievement — interpreting the works of Raymond De Gagnon for a benighted world.

"Surely, Mr. De Gagnon," I said mildly, "surely you do not place yourself in the same intellectual sphere with Albert Einstein."

De Gagnon regarded me with a gracious smile, breathing unobtrusively into his wispy white mustache.

"I dislike being immodest," he said, "but I have been called the most versatile genius since Leonardo da Vinci, the world's deepest thinker, the greatest dancer of all time, and the most intellectual painter."

"How is it," I inquired respectfully, "that you never became a city editor?"

"It's a funny thing," he replied. "I once wrote a play that an acquaintance of mine called the deepest ever written, a dream play which came to me while sleeping. I sent it to Stanley Kubrick, the noted film director, for possible production. Mr. Kubrick returned it without comment."

"To what do you attribute Kubrick's silence?" I asked.

"Jealousy," De Gagnon said. "There is no other way to explain it."

I inquired whether in his early period Mr. De Gagnon had revealed any mark of his ultimate omniscience.

"I would say my genius matured gradually," my companion explained. "I was born in Redwood Falls 69 years ago, moved to

Minneapolis at an early age and spent most of my working career as a haberdasher, shoe salesman and related activity.

"I retired several years ago and now live in an apartment at 1527 Hawthorne Avenue, a place which I would describe as comfortably cluttered. Among my mementoes is my crowning art work, a painting into which I have capsuled the mysteries of the universe into one small frame.

"My chief interest now, aside from dancing, is cosmology, in which I have propounded revolutionary theories to explain the relationship of space and matter. It takes us a few steps beyond Einstein.

"However, dancing remains my primary love. In informal competition I have danced against Hindus, Chinese, Japanese, Hawaiians, Poles, Negroes, and Russians, and beaten them all. Some people I have danced against, and some I have danced with. I really don't have a preference."

De Gagnon arose and padded to the juke box. His selection was a wailing saxophone rendition of "Melody of Love."

De Gagnon shuffled about languidly in his navy blue sweater and white work pants, recovering smoothly after being knocked off stride by a passing drunk.

Maneuvering past the bumper pool table, the dancer fluttered his arms in a largo tempo, giving the appearance of a man stalking a colony of sluggish butterflies or playing paddleball in slow motion.

Dazzled, I asked Mr. De Gagnon if he had ever danced professionally.

"I have trouble getting bookings," he acknowledged, "but I did get $2 once for appearing on television."

"But you have no resentment that your genius has thus far gone unrecognized?" I intruded.

"None. Beethoven wasn't accepted by everyone while he was alive. In that connection, I should tell you I am also a songwriter."

I stumbled into the sunlight, overwhelmed.

London in One (1) Day

THE TOWER OF LONDON — I am under heavy sedation and in the temporary care tonight of one of the tower's beef-eater's yeoman, who from time to time emerge from the labels of gin bottles to pull ax duty in this historic dungeon.

"This city," he tells me agelessly, "required more than a thousand years to build and the process — as you can see from the Honeywell building on the way to the airport — is continuing. It is the product of centuries of striving, bloodshed, building, scheming, plagues, wars, fires, and artistic genius. It covers hundreds of square miles and eons of history, and you, I understand, have attempted to see it all in one day."

"That is correct," I replied weakly. "They said it couldn't be done."

"And can it?"

"I would have made it," I said indomitably, "if it hadn't been for the language barrier. From the movies I was led to believe all Englishmen sound either like Lawrence Olivier or Elsa Lancaster."

"And you discovered?"

"Most of the ones I interrogated sounded like mandolin players from Naples. I walked three blocks from Victoria Station, asking directions most of the way, and all I got was, "You no speaka Italiano?"

"Yes, it is a pity," the beefeater commiserated. "The immigrants all make their contributions, but cannot tell directions without seeing the sun, and in London, this is disastrous."

"I beg your pardon," I corrected, "it is not the foreign language here but the English language that is the most difficult for me to comprehend. But you have asked me to chronicle my one-day saga in London as a historic document and I will comply."

To silence the purists immediately, I'll grant this is the classic illustration of how not to see London. But if your plane is leaving in the morning and your money is running out and you are convinced that on your next visit London will be the captive of long-haired guitar players and semi-nude schoolgirls, you will have to follow my directions.

Admitted, you are not so much making a tour as perpetrating it, but this is what you must do:

8 a.m. — Breakfast at your hotel. Allow 50 minutes for this seven-course meal, much of which will be edible. Drink all the tea available. If you like nothing else at table in London, you will thrive on the tea.

Breakfast over, make your preparation for a walk in London. Under no circumstances must you leave without an umbrella. If you do not have an umbrella, buy one. If the stores are not open, borrow one. If you cannot borrow one, steal one and make your explanations later to American Express. Next to a passport and interpreter, the umbrella is the indispensable fact of life here.

9 a.m. — Take the underground to Trafalgar Square. Keep your nerves under control. If you get lost in the cascades of escalators, remember the one sure direction to safety is up. Do not be alarmed by the swarming multitudes. That closed-circuit television screen there is monitored constantly on the surface, and announcers periodically will tell you which escalator to take to avoid suffocation.

The trains are efficient and numerous. The passengers are courteous. Do not let your last experience on the New York subway cow you into taking a cab.

9:30 a.m. — Enjoy Trafalgar and the Nelson Monument but do not loaf. Especially, do not be extravagant in your dole to the pigeons. Trafalgar pigeons are inclined to be rather slothful panhandlers, particularly under the Socialist Government. As an incidental note, in feeding the pigeons avoid squinting skyward whenever practicable.

11 a.m. — Stroll through St. James' Park in front of Buckingham Palace. You are walking in a routine London downpour but you may derive much from this excursion by imagining what it would be in the bi-monthly sunshine. Sip your fourth cup of tea at the little stand near the pond and try not to address the waitresses as "ducks."

Cross Buckingham Road carefully on your way to the changing of the guard. That little Austin zipping past you ignored the bobby's command to halt. Notice that the bobby is standing rigid, staring after the Austin. He is memorizing the license number. When you violate a traffic law in front of Buckingham Palace, you are asking not for a traffic ticket but a summons to the scaffold.

11:30 a.m. – They change the guard in the red clay compound before the royal palace, but as a concession to the cloudburst they bobtail the ceremony. It is an absolutely abominable day, yet there are 4,000 people watching through the black iron fence rails and 98 per cent of them are Londoners. Guard-changing in the rain is too serious a matter to be left to the tourists. The Londoner luxuriates in this condition wherein he is able to enjoy the misery of lousy weather in company with his countrymen.

12 noon – The imperishable face of Big Ben above you regards the world with its hands in an attitude of straight-up propriety. Ben is tolling noon, and assuredly all is right with the world and Pall Mall cigarettes.

12:30 p.m. – The Tower of London. We are standing on the scaffold plot where scores of the pious and profane were executed. Among them was the romantic Earl of Essex, reputed darling of Queen Elizabeth I and a man who allegedly died in dismay after learning that Errol Flynn was destined to get the part. Here also died Anne Boleyn, second wife of Henry VIII, who gained a snatch of immortality as an example of what can happen to a woman who uses too much tenderizer on the beef.

The crown jewels are here, the River Thames flows indestructibly beneath the Tower Bridge and London Bridge, and a busload of New Yorkers pushes forward insistently to see the ravens. If careful, you may hear the ghost of Sir Walter Raleigh sighing, "The Americans, back again. They have learned nothing since I dropped my coat in the mud back in Jersey."

1:30 p.m. – Westminster Abbey, the magnificent shrine of England. Across the street is Parliament, and Big Ben stands among the spires. The trouble with these buildings is that they are old. In Minneapolis, I am sure they would have gone the way of the Metropolitan Building and become part of shopper city.

3 p.m. – Leaving the Tower. You may pause for some contraband conversation with one of the scarlet-arrayed sentinels. "Yes," he says patiently, "it is a genuine bearskin hat, the pelt from Canada. It weighs approximately two pounds and when it is hot, mate, it is hot as hell."

3:30 p.m. – The Tube to Hyde Park at Marble Arch, the

celebrated Speakers' Corner on Sunday afternoon. This is the oratorical monkeys' island of the English-speaking world, wherein gather the crackpots, the free thinkers, free lovers, free-loaders, Communists, Fascists, anarchists and coffee-drinkers. All of them talk, some eloquently.

Occasionally there are fist fights. Always there is hostility and enraged language. The target today at most of the over-turned washtubs and fruit crates which serve as speakers' platforms are the rich and corrupt Americans. The target last week was rich and corrupt Americans. The target next week will be richer and corrupter Americans.

Here is George White, one of the speaking regulars, a droll, creased and weather-stained old man of 65, with all teeth missing except the two front ones. This gives him the appearance of an arthritic chipmunk. His regular audience of 500 includes at least 200 who have memorized every line of the same speech he has given for 15 years. They form a claque and chorus, finishing his sentences, flawlessly allowing time for dramatic pauses, heckling his lapses. George grins at the immaculate performance.

"I do not have time..." he says, "TO BE BRIEF," they respond. "I am too heavy..." he says, "FOR LIGHT WORK," they respond. "Too light..." "FOR HEAVY WORK," "and too sexy..." "FOR DAY WORK."

George is recalling the outbreak of World War II. "The bombs fell," he said, "and the government came after me. Sixteen million people in London and they wanted me to do the fighting. They examined me and said you have bad teeth. I said what the hell are you asking me to do, shoot the bloody Germans or eat them afterwards?" George drones for two more hours. They set clocks by him. If it's shorter or longer than two hours, they examine Big Ben, not George.

5:30 p.m. — The Tube to the Hotel for a change of clothes and a new umbrella. They are waiting with a cup of tea, the seventh of the day.

6:30 p.m. — Picadilly Circus, where you may see the latest in America's own cultural export, "The Return of the Magnificent Seven."

7:30 p.m. — Soho, the London Bohemia and clip joint sanctuary. You will find in the thin, erratic streets here some of the city's best food and a few of its more preposterous whores. The prostitutes in general have been moved off the streets, however, replaced by dirty movies that are advertised openly by signs and circus-type barkers.

9:30 p.m. — Back to that turreted symbol of the majesty of London, the Tower. It is closed for the night. An off-duty beefeater invites you to a pub to split a grog. I am weary, but still coherent. "Tell me, now," I say, "how DID you end up on the label of a gin bottle?"

"I'm surprised you did not know," he said, "that particular gin is made by an American company."

The beefeater was wrong, of course. The gin is as English as rain. "Yes," I told him, "I do love your city. As much as Rome, almost. But I am wet, and almost broke, and it is getting late and would you please . . ."

"Yes?"

"Take me to Pan-Am."

Kaat Pens a Letter

No doubt all American League zealots were delighted with Baltimore's four-game sweep over Los Angeles in the World Series, but the question now is:

Did it meet with Jim Kaat's approval?

Kaat is the Twins' pitcher who wants his organization to have a manager of whom the pitching coach can be proud. He is also one of the few pitchers in the majors who is campaigning for the job of secretary of state, and in support of his candidacy periodically publishes a sort of sweat-sock white paper to keep fans informed of events inside the clubhouse.

His first offering was intended to be a player's defense of Johnny Sain, the ousted Twins' pitching coach, but wound up closer to being a decapitation of Sam Mele, the manager.

I, too, regret that Sain is not going to be around to mother-hen the Twins' pitchers next season but have to assume that Kaat as a 25-game winner is large enough and old enough to survive the loneliness and deprivation.

Kaat's contention is that Sain was the most important genius in the organization, with the implied exception of Cal Griffith, who pays the salaries and is therefore exempt from the perils of Kaat's rating system.

I think you can make a case for a pitching coach or any coach winning a pennant, but not much of a case. I knew people who wanted to run Billy Martin last year for lieutenant governor (which from the size of the billboards around town clearly is the most coveted office in the state) for goading Zoilo Versalles into the Most Valuable Player award in 1965.

In fact, there was a sizable body of opinion which held that Martin, and not Zoilo, deserved the award. I have to disagree, in spite of my admiration for Martin's right hook and martini capacity. Billy may have been the most voluble but he really wasn't the most valuable.

You can see where the logic of this takes you. If you credit Martin with reforming Versalles and Sain with rehabilitating Mudcat Grant in 1965, you have to rap both of them for what happened to Versalles and Grant in 1966.

Nobody is going to challenge Jim Kaat's right to speak warmly of a man he admires and whom he credits with some of his own achievements. I would have expected, however, that he might have extended to Mele some of the magnanimity with which he caressed a fumbling teammate who cost him a ball-game in September.

If it was true that Sain was using Mele's hide for random gunnery practice, as other managers in the league maintain, he should have been kicked out not by Mele but by Griffith himself. And if the team's ranking pitcher is oblivious to the predicament of a manager trying to defend his bank account and reputation, I have to believe the pitcher's vision is obscured by the sight of 25 games on the Twins-O-Gram.

Griffith himself, of course, has been misused by the fans in the grand and sublime astigmatism of most of the fans' fraternity. He has been damned as a bumpkin, curmudgeon, mugwump and tee-totaler.

In fact, however, Griffith is an able baseball man and a freshly-dedicated Upper Midwesterner who, if he only had a speech-writer, would be the most exuberant missionary for the territory since Father Hennepin.

The one unsettling thing about Calvin is that he is reluctant to make a hero out of Sam Mele, whose record in the American League since 1962 is almost as good as Frank Robinson's.

There is some question whether Calvin is willing to concede that Mele is a major league manager, a year after nine other clubs in the league agreed unanimously.

This caution has led Calvin to do such things as cut the manager's pay publicly one year and by implication put him on probation for 1967 after he had finished first and second in consecutive seasons.

All of which mystifies me, inasmuch as the unemployment rolls and television booths are filled with managerial wizards who finished lower than Mele.

Or maybe Cal would prefer Eddie Stanky?

There He Was – No Goggles or Airspeed

Airplanes today travel from New York to London between meals, transport millions of people annually, provide commuter service for business and have become a condition of life for nations.

And yet as a theater of adventure, the air has not really surrendered the allure that has tantalized human beings since the beginning. Air travel may have become routine to millions but piloting has not, and the pilot's first flight – the novice's solo – retains the essence of jittery exhilaration it has always held.

—————

The runway was black and icy. It was 50 feet beneath the tri-cycled Cessna and moving toward me irrevocably.

There are certain mileposts of loneliness that chart a man's halting progress through life – when he is ambushed by a sudden bulge in the throat and stretches out for an encouraging hand only to discover an empty glove.

The first such time may be on his first date when, after a $15 dinner, he reaches for his wallet and finds he put on the wrong pants. Or, again, when he walks off the high board at night and learns in mid-descent that they have drained the pool.

To these might be added that smothering moment when the first-time flier realizes beyond escape that nobody in God's universe is going to put this plane down except himself or gravity, and gravity is impartial about what part of the plane gets down first.

In situations such as this, my thoughts unerringly follow a cycle in which I first ask myself, "How did I get into this?" – after which follows the even more meaningful question, "How am I going to get out of it?"

With the Cessna 150 skimming toward the runway at 75 miles an hour, the throttle phased down to 1,100 revolutions per minute and the ground coming up uncompromisingly, there just are not many alternatives.

In the lexicon of the football huddle, either you go for the touchdown here or perform the aeronautic equivalent of the quick kick, which is to goose the throttle and get out of there – a solution that may bring temporary relief, but will never get you into the end zone.

Far down the runway was the figure of a 27-year-old Iowan named Jerry Wilson, his hands jammed into his pockets against the cold. He had been in the cockpit with me a few minutes earlier as my flight instructor. I was struck by the glancing notion that Wilson looked much better beside me in the cockpit than out in all that cold air.

Wilson had left me with advice that was sound enough.

"Anything goes wrong," he said, "shove the throttle in and start climbing. The plane will fly at 50 miles an hour if it has to and, if it comes right down to it, the plane will just about fly itself if the pilot doesn't mess it up too much."

The miracle of powered flight is fraught with small humilities like this.

Wilson is an angular, twangy corn-belter, a professional pilot of high competence and barnyard drollness. He is employed by Fleet Air, Inc., a two-year-old flight training and charter service based at Flying Cloud Airport near Shakopee.

The field swarms with light plane traffic, evidence of a dramatic surge in private flying popularity over the past couple of years.

"We ought to be able to put you up there alone after eight air hours," speculated Fleet Air's Paul Barth, a former professional auto racer. "All you really need to learn how to fly is good depth perception, a little nerve and a good sense of which way the wind is blowing.

"At this point, it is hard to know whether you qualify on all counts, but since you have managed to get away from your employers in the middle of the day to come out here, the chances seem pretty good."

Barth conducted me on a pre-flight check of the saucy little Cessna, a 1,600-pound plane with a top speed of about 125 miles an hour, a 100-horsepower engine and that heady, chemical cabin aroma that lingers pleasantly in the nostrils.

Wilson slid into the cabin beside me. Within five minutes I was taxiing the plane down the flat-packed snow of the runway, groping with the rudders and uselessly turning the half-wheel of the aileron control in my hands as though it were the steering wheel of an automobile.

We chugged down the straightaway for a quarter of a mile and into the small furrow of a runway intersection. It was faintly exotic and richly exciting even on the ground, and you will not believe what happened next.

We got stuck in the snow at the runway intersection.

"How," Wilson asked with genuine wonderment, "did you find the one patch of snow on this airfield where we might get stuck?"

I shrugged sadly.

Wilson got out and swung the tail about.

"I don't suppose," I yelled miserably above the sound of the propeller, "it would do any good to rock the plane?"

"There is no way that is possible," Wilson said. "As you know, this plane does not have a reverse gear."

We got out of it with reasonable dispatch, however, and were airborne a few minutes later. Wilson maneuvered the plane in the gusts at 3,000 feet for 20 minutes and then turned over the controls to me for some banks and climbs. Later we practiced stall pullouts, touch-and-go landings and takeoffs and the following day forced landing procedures, more stall pullouts and more landings.

On the third day, after the eighth hour of instruction, Wilson handed me the key again and walked away.

There is no solitude quite like the solitude of an airplane cabin the moment you are left alone to fend for yourself.

I ran down the check list — carburetor heat, mixture, primer, ignition switch, throttle (open ¼), clear propeller area, starter handle (pull).

I pulled. The propeller was whirling. I looked into my right hand, and discovered somebody had placed the radio transmitter mike there, probably me. I turned on the radio switch and set the frequency at 121.7, prescribed for ground to tower communication.

Clearing my throat, I placed the microphone close to my mouth. I had a fleeting image of James Cagney doing this in some depression era movie out of my dim consciousness, and I was talking.

"Flying Cloud Control, this is Cessna 99 J at Fleet Air. Request instructions to taxi."

The disembodied voice of the tower came back in a torrent of settings and instructions, and I could not decipher any of them except the altimeter and the parting, "clear to taxi."

I hustled down the runway and turned the Cessna into the wind for the pre-takeoff check: Throttle setting at 1,700 rpm, engine instruments, magnetos. I was aware of what some of this meant, but not much.

The tower was talking again and clearing me for takeoff. I could not resist answering, "Niner, niner juliette, roger." The tower seemed pleased.

I swung the plane through the intersection, headed it into the wind, touched the throttle – and the engine died.

There was no way of determining the language of the men in the tower at this precise moment, but one has to assume it had imagination and texture.

There being nothing better to do, I started the engine again and raced down the runway. With the needle registering 65 miles an hour, I pulled back on the controls. At this speed, the plane is supposed to take off.

It took off.

"You are flying," I told myself. "Whatever happens five minutes from now when you try to land, at this exact flick of time you are flying."

There was time for no further congratulations because the Cessna was boring upward at an alarming angle and had to be brought under control. At an altimeter reading of 1,300, or about 400 feet off the ground, I banked 90 degrees to the left on a south heading, climbed another 400 feet, banked 90 degrees again and was flying parallel with the runway.

I now remembered to exhale.

Swinging the plane once more, I began gliding toward the runway, pulling back on the throttle to reduce power and trying to keep the plane's nose – what the lads in the trade call "the attitude of the nose" – elevated enough to control the airspeed. The wind was shoving me around. I ruddered and aileroned and throttled too much, I'm sure.

And now the runway was dead ahead.

"There are only two things that can really be bad for you on landing," Wilson had said, "if you don't get to the landing strip and if you land on your nose wheel."

I had the runway made, all right, but I was a little high. The plane was 50 feet over it now and I was trying to remember the attitude of the nose, the airspeed, the runway, the rudder, that lousy damn wind, and suddenly the runway was right here and the left wing was still down a little and then—

The wheels touched. At least a couple of them. And now they're all three there. The plane rolled blissfully for a while and then I jammed in the carburetor heat and throttle, took off again, landed with at least a grain of grace the second time and headed up for the third and final pass.

And for the first time I felt a nudge of pleasure. The sun was warm in my eyes, the countryside relaxed around me in its fresh-white symmetry. I removed my hand from the controls and the thing DID fly itself. With a pretension that might be pardoned, I whistled some aimless tune and I suddenly discovered I did not want to come down. The solitude was gay and amiable now, and the sky serene and buoyant.

It went a little better the third time down and I taxied across the field up to the Fleet Air hangar. With a calm that was totally insincere, I walked toward the company office and then bounded four steps at a time upstairs.

Wilson was there with Barth and owner Jim Ward. They smiled and shook my hand. Whereupon Wilson produced a pair of scissors, pulled out my shirt tail and snipped a section for the office bulletin board, the company ritual.

"You have soloed," Wilson said. "So now you can get about the business of learning how to fly."

The only things missing were the cognac and a pair of goggles.

Night of the Computers

Voters awoke on November 9, 1966 to discover that instant-result computers had removed most of the suspense and practically all of the blarney from election-night news coverage.

Engulfed by the GOP sweep, my favorite downtown street-cleaner — a Democrat — bayed sorrowfully at 6 a.m. today: "How do you like it, even the weatherman went Republican."

The only rational explanation for events of Tuesday night was that the computers were psychologically up for the game, tuned emotionally for a peak effort.

"I opened the lid of one of the 508's just before the polls closed," a CBS technician told me, "and brother, I mean those cog-wheels were two feet off the ground. You talk about being sky-high for the big one. I never saw anything keyed like that."

The machines made everybody obsolete — the man behind the microphone, the man behind the typewriter, the bartenders at the party rallies and even the politicians themselves. They undressed the defeated candidate of his one final and gallant dignity, the concession speech, which got to be outmoded along with the rest. Nobody made a victory claim. Voter profile analysis (VPA) did it for them, before the winners ever came out of the booths.

I'm not being envious. I truly marveled at the performance. VPA named Mondale the winner in Minnesota after two precincts had been reported, giving the Democratic senator an insurmountable lead in the tabulation, 31 votes to 15.

Ronald Reagan was anointed a winner by NBC before the makeup man arrived. CBS shifted to Soapy Williams' Michigan headquarters for a spot pick-up but heard him making sounds as though it still was a contest and put on a commercial. Williams was hopelessly out of date. VPA had elected Griffin 15 minutes earlier but nobody bothered to tell Soapy.

It was a dismal night, of course, for Minnesota Democrats, whose only real winner was the non-running Sandy Keith, who never got on the ballot.

Republicans were delirious except in the Mondale-Forsythe contest. I made my way through the bourbon gardens at the Holiday Inn Central last night and interrogated a Forsythe supporter.

"It's great for the rest of the ticket but looks bad for us," he admitted.

"Take heart," I replied. "You've still got a chance on EVE, RSVP, EVA and DIVCON."

"Well then, you better check WCTU," he said, "because somebody's beating the hell out of us."

Nobody, however, beat the computers, although for a while it appeared Minnesota was going to get no worse than a draw.

Two minutes after the polls closed VPA elected Mondale. At 9:13 p.m., ABC radio elected Rolvaag, who was running 20,000 votes ahead of LeVander at the time. A few minutes later, however, CBS said it looked like LeVander. At about this time the resident oracle on channel 5, Dr. G. T. Mitau, was saying that despite the Rolvaag lead it looked like LeVander 53.3 per cent and Rolvaag 46.7.

Channel 4's Dave Moore and George Rice dutifully reported the CBS declaration for Rolvaag, but weren't quite convinced, and nobody who has done the dressing room piece on Minnesota elections is going to blame them. "Our figures," Moore said tentatively, "don't quite jibe with that." Mitau seemed faintly apologetic himself. At this point it was a horse race between Moore and Mitau.

Five minutes later radio reported that the computers disagreed. One gave it to Rolvaag and the other to LeVander. One more machine and the Socialist candidate would have been in the running. As it was, the only TV celebrity around here who wasn't upstaged by the computers was Van Brocklin.

The computers, sadly, snookered the thoroughly wise and honorable Eric Sevareid, who got caught between backlash and frontlash and vote projections and ultimately turned to Walter Cronkite with a brave smile and said, "Walter, I'm out of wisdom."

But this time the computers had ignominiously outflanked Mayor Daley of Chicago, who hates computers and who had tried to snarl the network vote projection by holding out Chicago precincts. The networks elected Percy anyway, explaining they had run around Daley, which I assume was a form of dashlash.

Set 'Em Up in Baltimore

BALTIMORE, Md. – I had a premonition of disaster in Baltimore when I ordered a glass of water in a downtown bar and was billed $1.35.

"I didn't insist on ice cubes," I protested.

"Mister," the barmaid said tolerantly, "I'm sorry about that charge but we just can't have people here watching the strip show and drinking water."

Which, of course, set me seething. "As you can see," I explained, "I'm here playing big brother for an insomniac buddy who wanted a nightcap. I don't want any booze and I don't trust your coffee. All I asked was a glass of water. For a buck thirty-five I could hire the cook."

What I mean is that $1.35 is a hellish markup for any glass of water, whether it comes from Chesapeake Bay or Lady Baltimore's bathtub.

But you just have to condition yourself to that kind of over-the-counter surgery in Baltimore, which as a city is a kind of sociological misfortune, the Jukes family of seaboard society, a droopy-pantsed troll with a lingering trace of halitosis and some small genius for usury.

The Viking stay overnight in Baltimore was at a fading mausoleum called the Sheraton-Belvedere (which is the kind of place George Washington rejected before he tried Valley Forge).

The hotel charged me 40 cents for a cup of coffee and re-fill. "There must be some mistake," I observed to the waitress. "Obviously these are World Series prices. I would like to talk to Mr. Sheraton or, at the very least, Mr. Belvedere."

"No," she replied sadly, "I'm afraid these are our standard prices and simply are not negotiable, with or without cream."

It cannot be said the visitor is allowed to enter without warning. The most prominent landmark in town at night is a tower surmounted by a large sign reading "Bromo Seltzer," which I take it is some type of neoned prophecy of the hours ahead.

In view of these circumstances, therefore, one does not want to berate the Vikings too harshly for events of the final minutes in Memorial Stadium here Sunday.

I'm sure you know by now that there was a degree of misunderstanding about what course to pursue on the final play of the game, whether it ought to be a field goal or a forward pass.

In this situation, one is inclined to be charitable. In other words, with the Vikings you don't necessarily insist on total unanimity between the high command on the bench and the combatants on the field.

All you ask is some sort of working concensus, the object of which is to get the football off the hash marks and in play before the siren goes off.

Regrettably, our forces got caught in the switches and milled about in a general sort of way at the Baltimore 35-yard line. As a result, the lineup on the final play resembled the state DFL convention, and the game ending in the midst of this vague formation.

So the Vikings lost, but you are going to get no condemnation of Francis Tarkenton from me.

I have heard Tarkenton blamed for throwing in the middle of the field, for not stopping the clock with a pass with 15 men on the field in the last minute, for not removing the offense in favor of the field-goal team, and for other unidentified transgressions.

My only observation on this is that he must have had help.

In any case, it was a suitable climax for the week-end. I spent a couple of hours in Ann Arbor Saturday afternoon watching the University of Michigan test-run its new computers against Minnesota.

I wouldn't contend that Michigan's Bump Elliott ran up the score, even though it ended 49-0 and Michigan got one of its first-string linebackers maimed in a last-ditch stand against a Minnesota drive at a time when Michigan led by seven touchdowns.

My guess is that anyone who would lose three games with a team like Michigan's is entitled to a lapse of memory.

Unionizing the Bedroom

Instinctively I squirmed Friday before reporting a market expert's estimate that 50-million American women are organized in some fashion or other.

I was sure it would somehow touch a light to the fraternal passions of Antonio G. Felicetta, the well-manicured local Teamster road runner who is constantly on the prowl for new membership in his union.

Not unexpectedly, my telephone rang. The voice announced itself as that of Antonio G. Felicetta.

"What's this business about organized women?" Felicetta inquired. "And why haven't we got our share in the Teamsters?"

I explained that the report referred not necessarily to unionized women but to the combined membership in civic clubs, social clubs, sewing clubs, Mothers for Cassius Clay, Co-eds for Christine Keeler, and similar organizations.

From the unnatural pause on the other end, I was convinced a bold scheme was flowering beneath the smoke shroud of Felicetta's cigar.

"I'm afraid of what you're going to suggest," I said.

"Well, what's wrong with it?" he countered. "More people are being unionized every day. I understand even school kids are getting into it. What's wrong with unionizing the American housewife?"

I declined to be stampeded.

"Tony," I said, "you're okay with truck drivers but you have flopped so far in your plans to unionize pro football players, lion-tamers, and Cal Griffith's relatives.

"Besides, I want to remind you that the idea of a women's union isn't entirely new. It was spawned 2,000 years ago, which was even before Dave Beck, by a Greek playwright named Aristophanes."

"I'm not prejudiced," Felicetta said temperately. "I think it's possible to be a Greek and still be a good Teamster."

"Aristophanes," I continued, "wasn't a Teamster. He wrote a play called Lysistrata, the crux of which was that the women of the time were tired of batching it while their husbands went off to throw spears at each other in some bush league war.

"So they got together and decided to withhold their favors from the men until they stopped the spear-throwing."

"What's this 'withhold their favors' stuff?" Felicetta wanted to know.

"They gave them the cold shoulder," I elaborated. "In other words, no truce, no smooch."

"I get it," Felicetta said, "a lockout."

"Lockout, closed shop, whatever you want to use. Anyhow, it worked, naturally, one of the first recorded cases of enlightened unionism in action."

Felicetta paused again to weigh the implications of this. It was apparent that he was being torn between the unionist's code of ethics and the compassion any man feels at the sight of a browbeaten buddy.

"It would have been tough on those women if the guys brought in some strikebreaking floozies," he said absently.

"Surely, you of all people wouldn't condone scabbery in any form to break up a strike," I lectured.

"No, I guess you're right. But there's still something to be said about a housewives' union, especially the fringe benefits like so much time away from the kids each year, Christmas bonuses, the husband's really got to help with the dishes instead of showing off for the neighbors, things like that."

"You're a union man, not a reformer," I reminded him. "And what happens if the guys don't want to cooperate in this little utopia?"

"The thing that what's-his-name wrote about, you think it could happen here, huh?"

"I think there's a real danger."

Felicetta sighed, subdued.

"It's not worth the risk. I think I'll try recruiting those lion-tamers again."

Don't Rush the Slush

Somewhere in this town a cab driver with a curse on his head is breathing the free, monoxided air while more deserving men – stranglers, tip-snatchers, and embezzlers – moulder in jail.

I have agents prowling the streets and alleys. Descriptions have been sent to hotel doormen, all-night bakeries and random drunks. We are going to track this man and bring him to book.

I say we, although I am involved in this only on humanitarian grounds and as a private evangelist against the most loathsome traffic offender of all, the slush-musher.

It is hard to predict when the season is going to open. But there is one day every year when all restraints come unglued, when auto drivers are seized by a mass mania to plow through puddles of ice water and deface their innocent brothers, the pedestrians.

Veteran pedestrians refer to this as Mush in the Slush Day, comparable in its aimless hysteria to Bonus Stamp Day at the little super, the ice breakup on the Yukon, and the day they run the bulls in Spain.

I usually observe the phenomenon at a suburban parking lot, where the cars have more maneuverability and thus are able to develop more thrust plunging through the slush than they can downtown.

Wednesday I had no such option. Running low on fuel, I left my car with my service station attendant with instructions to fill the tank.

I returned in mid-afternoon and plucked the bill from my steering wheel. It read $9 for a tankful of gasoline. It was a round, clean, and horrifying figure. Friends, my automobile is not all that big. There was no reason to doubt the honesty of the arithmetic, although at those prices a man ought to be getting helium instead of petroleum.

It was the first time I have had to make a down payment on a tank of gasoline. It also impelled me in the direction of Twin City Federal to make a withdrawal for the balance of the payment, and thus I was afoot downtown when the opening day of slushing season turned on the strollers with its full cubic power.

Crossing Marquette on 8th Street, I looked up to see a lone pedestrian standing on the corner waiting for the light. I looked beyond him, and froze in the mucky ruts.

A Blue and White cab was streaming down the street at destroyer speed, emitting a 10-foot-high coxcomb of sludge-water in its wake.

You could pick out the cabbie's course by the synchronized panic of the sidewalk mobs. In unison they rushed to the protecting walls of the commerce buildings, like trained marines dropping for survival against strafing planes.

Momentarily, I gazed at that long, slim, dirty geyser behind the cab, admiring the cruel beauty of it. And then I remembered the pedestrian, standing there in a stylish new coat that appeared to be cashmere.

"Look out," I screamed. "The slush."

And then, terrified, he saw it. Too late. The slush was on him now, thickly, splatteringly, and undrycleanably. It looked as though the men from Roto Rooter had just surfaced.

I went up to him to offer my hand. The poor man was spluttering inarticulately but by card he identified himself as Vince E. Williams, bakery accounts manager of the Pillsbury Company.

At this precise moment we heard a muffled shout of alarm behind us. "Look out," somebody was yelling, "here they come again." It was a green and white Central Avenue bus this time, churning resolutely.

There were five of us on the corner now. With the self-preservation instinct implanted in the human animal before the dawn of history, we linked arms in this moment of deepest peril and lurched toward the wall.

Clinging to the plate glass, we spread-eagled ourselves. We heard that ominous "whoosh" as the sludge descended on the sidewalk, but breathed again when it fell short by a foot. One dirty chunk would have gotten us all.

By this time there was screeching in the streets, as though the monster of the black lagoon had appeared above the Foshay Tower. Eventually it quieted, and there is calm again today.

I don't really know what can be done about the mushers. But it might be that the city should establish some kind of special compensation for the victims. For a name, I have a suggestion, and I thought you'd never ask.

A slush fund. What else?

Tie One for the Gipper

EAST LANSING, MICH. — I have asked the hospital laboratory people across the street to ship a supply of sedative this morning to Knute Rockne in care of his personal suite in Valhalla.

My contention is that Rockne needs some kind of booster today after watching Notre Dame sue for a truce in the final minute of its game with Michigan State at East Lansing Saturday.

Doubtless you observed the remarkable spectacle through the magic of electronics — Notre Dame refusing to throw the football in a touchdown attempt during the final minute when it had the opportunity to win the solar system's game of the year.

Notre Dame at the time was ranked No. 1, Michigan State No. 2. The score was tied and Notre Dame was in possession on its 30-yard line. At this point the champs wanted the game to expire with dignity and without a settlement. Embarrassingly, Michigan State kept calling time out.

My chief objection to all of this is not that Notre Dame is an overly-inflated football team, which it is not, or that Ara Parseghian is not a good coach, which he is. I was not all that impressed by Michigan State, which seemed Saturday to have more post-game orators on its roster than All-Americans.

I was saddened, however, by the tortured morass of the Notre Dame coach's logic which seemed to convert his splendid football players from baritones to fluttery sopranos in the eyes of the viewing public. It was like the board chairman of Hertz saying to the board chairman of Avis, "Okay, I'll split with you. We'll settle for being 1½."

Whatever faith Parseghian has in the erudition and fidelity of people who take part in football polls, it is greater than mine. I used to do it weekly for the Associated Press several years ago. The barber down the street saw as much football — probably more, because I was extracting slivers in the Memorial Stadium press box Saturday afternoons while the barber was switching channels.

The point is that polls, mythical championships and some half-warm gratification in not losing the big game are not really adequate to match the coach's larger responsibility to his football team. This responsibility is no different in front of 30 million televiewers than it is on the playground – and that is to try to win the ball game, whether it's at 2 o'clock or 4.

I would guess it is doubly painful for Notre Dame under these circumstances because of its heritage, and because this game of all demanded a kind of historic sense, dimension and presence, if there are such things in football stadiums. Regretfully, Notre Dame was grubbing and self-demeaning at the finish and my sympathies go with the ballplayers.

In any case, it may spawn a new tradition. It is possible to visualize Coach Ara in some future halftime sermon, exhorting his players "to go out there, when the going gets toughest, and tie one for the Gipper."

And if George Gipp was really the heller old Notre Damers say he was – before Ronald Reagan resuscitated him as the kid next door – I'm sure the Gipper will reply: "What I actually said, Ara, was to tie one ON for the Gipper."

I acknowledge, however, being bothered less by Notre Dame's last-minute timidity than the casual obscenity in some sections of the stadium here. There were 20-foot long banners being paraded in the stands that would not have been allowed on the Buddy Hackett show. As an exercise in slobbiness, it was the kind of sight to make one forgive the town of Baltimore for its garden-variety social offenses.

The ball game, of course, was first-rate and savagely waged, although it was somewhat tedious in the second half. I found myself glancing through the rosters and being amused in retrospect by the published remarks two weeks ago of an alumni blow-hard in Minneapolis who doesn't like pros, partly because they are supposed to be transients.

Notre Dame, probably for understandable reasons, is the only school in the country which equips its talent scouts with Rand-McNally yearbooks.

Michigan State is even more imaginative. The Spartans get student athletes from not only Texas, where most respectable Big Ten schools like Minnesota go, but Hawaii and the South Seas as well. Michigan State, accordingly, equips its scouts with surf-boards and tridents.

State scouts can proudly claim to be the only ones in the country who cross the international dateline for halfbacks.

A Night in the Tank

In mimeographed instructions handed to each new inmate, the superintendent of the Minneapolis City Workhouse states, "This may be one of the blackest days of your life." A man entering jail may do so with shame, loathing, or defiance. Whatever his attitude, it is a day he will never forget.

The writer had himself booked and jailed, and for four days lived among the inmates of the city jail and workhouse, his identity unknown to them. This article, based on his experience, reveals what might happen if you went to jail.

———

The greasy cream-and-gray walls of the Minneapolis city jail detention cell are smeared with obscenities, the ragpicking literature of the social misfit.

On one wall is painted a red rose of spectacular vulgarity, imparting some alien and lonely color to the shabbiness of the cell.

The place is strewn with fallen-down drunks. They are sleeping off their jags on the dirty tiled floor in the main cellroom or on skinny, board-flat bunks in the eight single cells — all part of the barred complex called "the tank."

This is where the city holds misdemeanor suspects who cannot put up bail or who are waiting for it to arrive.

The turnkey opens the iron gate and nudges a suspect, newly booked, into the common cell. The air is warm and rancid. It smells of wine and tobacco and, in some of the corners, of men who have been sick over their clothes or over their floormates.

There are 30 men in the fifth floor cell tonight, a Saturday night, floating-sideshow night in the city jail.

Most of them are panhandling lushes, whining deadheads for whom the most important fact of life at the moment is cadging a cigarette from the bum who got lucky and stole a pack from another bum, who was unconscious from drinking.

The place is lit a hazy pale yellow. Save for the eight rude cots, there is no place to sit or sleep except the floor. There is a washbowl and drinking faucet in the cell nearest the locked doorgate, and a coverless toilet bowl stands above a thicket of crumpled cigarette packages and refuse in each of the cells.

For the first-timer it is a jolt — not from the treatment he gets, because this is likely to be civilized, within reason.

It comes, instead, from the sights and sounds and smells; but beyond this — if he has any sense of regret — is the smothering humiliation of being thrown behind bars and being counted with the crackling and rotten-toothed old wino propped up against the wall.

The cell door is opened and a beefy young man in a gray topcoat, a blue suit and rumpled hair enters. The jailer tells him he can make a telephone call at the end of the corridor in a few minutes; and that if he has to, he may make another later at night.

The jailer is taking the part of the light-hearted usher tonight, doing a variety act with his intramural gags and getting a noisy, bloodshot response from the drunken audience.

The new inmate's face is florid and disturbed. He is resentful but too worried to be arrogant. He may have been careless with his automobile, or he may have been careless at the bar before getting into his automobile, or he may have written a bad check, or told a cop where he could go.

The cell incumbents who are awake — slouched on the floor or lying on the bunks or standing around dragging on cigarettes — look up and give the newcomer 10 seconds of their valuable attention before returning to the earnest business of killing time.

He walks into the bunkless main cellroom and accidentally brushes one of the derelicts who is still standing. Involuntarily, he whisks off the coat sleeve that made contact.

One of the vagrants notices and snickers, "What the hell was you expecting, a ballroom? You may as well plunk down, because you ain't no different than the rest of us."

The new man tells him to go to hell and mind his own business. He makes his phone call a few minutes later, is returned to the cell and sits down against a wall, his face buried unreadably in the crook of his elbow, resting on his knee.

It is silent here now except for the occasional squeak of a pair of shoes heading for a cell toilet, indistinct voices and sporadic laughter in the police quarters off the corridor, and the adolescent voice of a 19-year-old tough who is dominating a four-man huddle in one of the cells.

The punk is proud of his wavy black hair and heavy chest and cannot keep the comb off his scalp nor his right hand from playing with the buttons of his open shirt.

The three to whom he is talking are there on driving charges, for auto theft and a string of traffic violations.

"All I asked the guy was for a quarter," he is saying. "What a creep, the guy. I think he was a fairy. He had to be, the way he talked. I needed the quarter for a bus ride."

I walked over to the group and asked the young tough what happened.

"What happened was he said he didn't want to give me any money. So I slugged him, right there in front of the Radisson ramp. Somebody called a cop and they picked me up.

"The guy hit his head, I guess. Anyhow, I really banged him. They come and took him to the hospital. I don't want to see no harm come to the guy, but I did hit him a pretty wallop."

I asked why he struck the man.

"Hell, I was boiled drunk. What else?"

He is enjoying his momentary celebrity here, more sure of himself now with a sympathetic and respectful audience. He bites his lip rhythmically, as others would crack their fingers. He is thinking about the courtroom Monday, and one has the impression he would not object to a grown-up, big-time sentence from the judge.

The jailer opens the gate and makes a quick, breezy tour of the cell, twisting a dozing drunk's head away from the mess he has made on the floor.

At six in the morning an old man with a cart passes free coffee and sweet rolls through the bars. One of the auto suspects slips into the back of the line for a second handout, but the old man recognizes him and tells him to get lost.

Even in jail the chiselers are still trying.

(signed): Anxious Abby

Her message was provocative and urgent and seemed to spring from the depths of a troubled woman's heart.

"My problem," she informed me, "is that I simply cannot take off six pounds of excess weight. It bothers my peace of mind because I know I have will power."

The distressed lady identified herself unpretentiously as "Abby."

Instinctively, I grasped that here was a person whose problem was too pressing and intimate to come within the scope of the newspaper's resident lovelorn counselor. It required a special kind of spontaneous and imaginative care, and besides this she had not included a stamped, self-addressed envelope.

"Ah, my dear Abby Van Buren," I said. "You look radiant and autumnal standing there in your riotous tangerine outfit and fedora-style hat."

"Why thank you," she said sweetly. "It was just something I picked off the rack. Shall we drive to my apartment or do you intend to hitch-hike?"

Miss Van Buren's voice has a deep and casually cultivated resonance that seems strange emerging from a lady so tiny; a voice that bespeaks the green-tasseled sweep of the Iowa prairie of her childhood; a sound I would characterize as alfalfa alto and Marshalltown mezzo-soprano.

"Ab," I said solicitously, "what is this nonsense about a diet problem? You can't weigh more than 102 pounds and look trim, chic and diminutive."

"The problem," she confided, "is I have never been excited about exercise sports like skiing, touch football and calisthenics. My idea of hard exercise is to open the window and chew gum vigorously."

I decided to adopt an attitude of paternal patience toward this very engaging woman, wheeled my automobile in front of the Towers Apartments and smoothly opened the car door for her. "We are here," I announced. "Very good," Miss Van Buren observed, "you have missed my place by eight miles."

My veneer of silken urbanity began wilting at this point and Miss Van Buren swung onto the offensive, second-guessing outrageously as we blundered through the late-afternoon traffic toward the River Drive apartments where she lives.

"Aren't you the guy who is supposed to have his personal traffic consultant instead of a psychiatrist to ease him through the trauma of Minneapolis traffic?" she asked.

"That is correct," I said.

"Honey," she replied, "I don't often advise people voluntarily, but the way you drive this traffic you either need a compass, a priest, or a new traffic consultant."

The high-altitude apartment suite where Miss Van Buren lives with her businessman-husband, Mort Phillips, imparts a subtle sense of calm, unrushed millions. It is tasteful, paneled, portraited and roomy in the way the Smithsonian is roomy.

One sinks effortlessly to his ankles as he progresses through Abby's red-carpeted office, which is efficiently furnished with copy typewriters, speech typewriters, electric typewriters, tape recorders and stereos.

In addition, I would have sworn I saw a Chinese cookie jar from which Miss Van Buren must occasionally crib a Chinese fortune for use when her oracular powers momentarily wane.

The door opened and a happy maid named Gisela brought in a cherry cheesecake Dear Abby had baked for her husband. "Ab," I said sorrowfully, "the cheesecake is delicious but very caloric. The only way you can trim off a few pounds is simply to refuse to consider eating this stuff. And now, please, get your fingers out of the platter."

The phone interrupted this monologue and Abby was purring adoringly into it, "Yes, my dear sweetheart; yes, dear, just as you wanted it; honey, it is so good to hear your voice again."

Unlike Miss Van Buren's mailman, Phillips never has to ring twice.

The Rollicking Ranger Named Mariucci

The demise of John Mariucci as hockey coach at the University of Minnesota can only be interpreted by the town's culture-lovers as a blow comparable with the sacking of the old Metropolitan Building.

I consider it the unhappiest event on campus since the construction of Memorial Stadium or the eviction of McCosh from his book store.

I take this position because there is something utterly, originally and unquenchably civilized about Mariucci, something like old Chianti at a ravioli-fest.

It's not quite clear whether Mariucci resigned or was removed, and you can dismiss the official explanation as fluff, but I regard this as irrelevant in any case.

What I'm worried about is the panic that has been sowed suddenly among program chairmen from the Minneapolis Woman's Club to the Kiwanians in Baudette.

Who ever heard of a midwinter beef and applesauce social without Mariucci as the principal orator? Who ever heard of Kundla without Mariucci? For that matter, who ever heard of Chianti without Mariucci?

It is plain we have here a cultural crisis in the community. Reub Youngdahl's annual turkey banquet is in jeopardy because I'm not sure that Youngdahl, Warmath, Griffith, Kundla and Sid Hartman can handle it alone without Mariucci.

The logical consequence of this is that the Lutherans may have to petition the university for a reconsideration.

Even more distressing, however, is the damage wrought to the flowering television career of Glen Reed, the university's assistant athletic director, whose ratings used to zoom whenever he put Mariucci on at halftime.

Mariucci, as you remember, used to make some comfortable pizza money by harpooning the sport of basketball, which is eminently harpoonable.

At a dull moment during the 1966 high school basketball tournament, Reed got Mariucci in front of a camera and asked the irreverent warrior how he viewed the proceedings.

Mariucci glommed the cue effortlessly. "I find basketball," he said, "as exciting as watching two old men fish."

The only way Reed can possibly maintain that level of class and style on his show next year is to retain Dr. Athelstan Spilhaus of the Institute of Technology, who now must succeed Mariucci as the resident raconteur on campus.

Mariucci, of course, has assiduously cultivated his image as the front-man for some kind of mythical, locker room Mafia, but he has a native intelligence which goes well beyond that of most of his detractors — who are not many — and a basic, physical courage that is surpassed by none of them.

He demonstrated it for years as a hockey player at a time when Canadians were trying to run him out of the league, and there are scores of people in this town who are in his debt by reason of his bedrock humanity.

For all of that, he is a son of nature who has spawned a special literature from the casual, harmless vulgarity of the athletic breed to whom the worst sin is phoniness.

I remember Mariucci presiding over an annual meeting of hockey coaches, trying aimlessly to maintain Roberts' Rules of Order in the face of babbling strife.

Somebody put forward a motion. This was followed by a clatter of debate which seemed to Mariucci superfluous.

"The hell with speeches," Mariucci announced. "Somebody second the goddamn motion."

I have no doubt that the university hockey team, under a promising new coach named Glen Sonmor, will continue to win more than it loses, as it did under Mariucci, and will win a title now and then, as it did under Mariucci.

I regret, however, that they may have to change the tint of the Williams Arena ice from Mariucci's favorite creme de menthe green to ginger ale amber.

Like the rest of us, John is an imperfect human being. I don't think he has ever had to suffer the conscience of hypocrisy, however, and he is a man for that.

It has been a pleasure to know him and to call him friend.

Why Deputize the Ladies?

For more than 20 years society has struggled nervously with the problem of harnessing the power of the atom. The idea is to use it in such a way that we will not all be blown to hell before the next tax raise.

It may be unfair and premature, therefore, to ask that somebody ought to get around now to harnessing a far more combustible energy — the unpredictable impulses of organized womanhood.

I think it's silly shadow-boxing to argue whether women rule the world. As long as they run the family budget, what happens in the United Nations is never going to seem very urgent or permanent. The old man may figure he decides where the government spends its millions, but it's the woman who decides where he spends his time.

So she has all this power and influence. Her natural instinct — once she has failed to reform her husband — is to reform the world.

In this community, we have given her a hatpin as a form of sidearm, which is all right as far as it goes, meaning 2¾ inches by latest measurement.

I don't object to this, nor do I object to the campaign of the Minneapolis Chamber of Commerce women's division to help the police by making citizens more alert to the crime dangers around them.

Granted, crime in the cities is a serious problem, of mounting complications. The question is: Do we really want to deputize everybody in the neighborhood?

I am baring my soul in this fashion because of a visit last week from Mrs. Virgille L. Peeke, the chairwoman of the chamber women's division, and Police Inspector Donald Dwyer, who is a truly galahadian figure in his silver hair, brass badge, and green necktie, and no doubt a knight errant to hundreds of members of Mrs. Peeke's hatpin brigade.

Mrs. Peeke wants to pump up publicity for the appearance next week of Mrs. Margaret Moore, who led a similar crusade in Indianapolis. She wants all of us to be ex-officio patrolmen, reporting suspicious behavior, scrupulously protecting our own property and being ready to jab any assailant with a hatpin, which is the group's badge and lodge symbol.

Again, with most of these goals I agree. I think the chamber women might render a more effective service, however, by throwing their restless energy and their husbands' commercial influence into a campaign to add about 100 patrolmen to the police force, which Dwyer needs more than hatpins.

Very earnestly, I would like to see amateurs down the block stay out of police work, even though Dwyer argues they are needed. An angry neighbor or a hemmed-in motorist is not always the most reliable informant. And there are few forces on earth as formidable as misdirected piety. When the soft-headed and the malicious become detectives, we are truly headed for large problems and, inevitably, false arrest.

But when Dwyer and Mrs. Peeke talk about people getting tougher in looking after themselves, I am with them completely.

"Few people are aware," Dwyer said, "that the solicitor they're talking to at the door may actually be a break-in broker who gets 10 per cent commission from the burglar for casing the house. If you're doubtful about the solicitor, ask for identification. If he pussy-foots, call the police. If he's heading out in a hurry, get his license number.

"When you drive, keep your car doors locked all the time. When you're away from home, keep your doors and windows locked and dead-bolt the doors. If you're away for an evening only, draw the drapes and leave several lights burning. If you're away for a longer period, leave the drapes open but pull the shades in one or two rooms and leave a light in the bathroom.

"Never walk alone after dark, choose well-lighted streets and don't wear enticing or flamboyant clothing when out alone late.

"And if you are a woman and you are grabbed, jab your hatpin at whatever part of the attacker's anatomy is exposed and scream like hell. If you don't have a hatpin, just scream like hell."

All right, good. But I would rather not turn the coffee klatch into a posse.

Demise of the Dagmars

We are graced this weekend by the presence of that level-chested lass from England, Twiggy, who is supposed to be the culminating stroke of 10,000 years of female development.

In the sad-eyed view of the lads in this office, Twiggy is not so much a stroke as a total collapse. This is regrettable, because the typical male had come to feel great pride in the progress women had been making over the years and was convinced they had rounded the corner with the arrival some seasons ago of the prodigiously contoured Dagmar.

It is superfluous to note they just don't make women like Dagmar anymore. It may be true that the lady in her prime had some of the noisy qualities of the hillbilly square dance caller, that she got her cultural breeding too close to Baltimore, that she breakfasted on frankfurters, and that her voice had that gently abrasive quality which identifies a laryngitis victim trying to lick a hangover.

In short, you could fault Dagmar for a certain amount of forgiveable slobbiness, but you could never complain about her silhouette. There was a distinctiveness to her movements as she walked, a kind of suspended vitality.

Dagmar may have left you with some doubt as to her destination, but as viewed in full gear, there was absolutely no doubt about which direction she was moving in.

Twiggy, on the other hand, leaves one wondering whether we are viewing a woman or a protest movement.

I'm sure she is an extremely fetching young lady and well-mannered and deserving. My only objection to her making a few million dollars is the precedent she is setting. There are certain things that look agreeable in a concave outline, but a woman is not one of them. And if she is, not only the designers but all of us are ready for the river.

My judgment is that Twiggy needs a square meal and an elastic exerciser more than an agent.

The real danger to a well-adjusted civilization, of course, is that we may suddenly find the streets swarming with Twiggies wearing minirompers, large eyes, short hair and the first stage of malnutritive pallor.

It took the British 200 years to avenge the Boston Tea Party, but with the creation of Twiggy they are now finally managing. Science has never been able to do much about the process of natural selection. The fashion experts are starting to succeed at it, however, gradually bringing us to the point where it is difficult to determine who is selecting what.

All of which tells us what can happen to humanity if you read the wrong fashion magazines or get hooked on the wrong diets. It also means I am going to recant what I have been telling women about slimming.

By a quirk of coincidence, I have in the mail today a diet sent to me by a woman in Robbinsdale and described as "the new Mayo Clinic diet."

Alleged "Mayo Clinic" diets have been making the rounds for years and are, by and large, frauds. The clinic itself classifies so-called "egg diets" and "two-week" diets as bizarre and disowns any authorship of them.

The one at my fingertips prescribes:

Breakfast — ½ grapefruit, 2 eggs any style, minimum of 2 slices of bacon and you may eat as much bacon and eggs as you want, 12 or more if you wish.

Lunch — ½ grapefruit, meat of any kind, style or amount, and as much salad as you can eat, with any dressing.

Dinner — ½ grapefruit, meat or fish of any style or amount, gravy without flour and green, yellow or red vegetables.

I agree this does not look like a diet. It looks, instead, like the First Infantry Division's Christmas menu. The Mayo Clinic says it is so much wishful thinking.

But I am recommending it to women who want the satisfaction of dieting without losing any weight.

In this town, at least, I think the Twiggies ought to leaf out.

The Democratic Daytons

Most of us have lived long and agreeably with the remarkable family known as the Daytons, and have a charge-a-plate to prove it.

We wear this not as a credit card but as a badge of respectability, a passport to the company's wondrous and revolving-charge Persian markets from Nicollet to Rochester.

From the various members of the clan we have come to expect a high degree of fearlessness, leadership, zeal and a few 99-cent sales now and then. The Daytons, in fact, have succeeded at almost everything they have attempted except – so far, at least – the Nicollet Mall. Even that troubled project is making headway and no longer qualifies as a disaster area, although it remains the most expensive sandbox in the state.

In view of the Daytons' well-established class and reasonableness, therefore, I was not surprised when the company's publicity department produced promptly on request an analysis of the handwriting of George D. Dayton II, as performed by the Anavac computer on the first floor downtown.

For some time now the company has been entertaining its customers with this futuristic gadget, casually intercepting them in their orderly march to the cash register and thus beating the State Fair action by a couple of weeks. The machine pretends to perform a personality analysis of the subject, based on his signature.

Viewed purely as fun-and-games, the machine deserves high ratings. As an electronic swami, however, I would put it down as an impishly harmless fraud which may or may not be worth 75 cents a throw, depending on how desperately you need a psychiatrist.

I tried it a couple of times, compared it with competitors, and have concluded the machine needs a couch more than its customers. In short, the computer has a split personality.

Accompanied by one of the town's more reputable attorneys, I submitted my signature twice, making the penmanship as close to identical as I could.

On the basis of the first signature, the machine decided I was, among other things, reliable, sincere, inclined to procrastinate, courageous, inhibited, aloof, and attractive to the opposite sex.

On the basis of the second signature the machine classified me as forgetful and careless, emotionally mature, positive and self-reliant, sentimental, easily-influenced, self-composed and attractive to the opposite sex.

You will conclude immediately it is almost impossible to be all those things simultaneously and still stay out of the hospital, jail, or Joe Pyne's interview room. You will also notice one constant here is attractiveness to the opposite sex, on which practically every customer scores high. The machine thus falls into the operating pattern trail-blazed by the earliest psychologists: It may be erratic but you can't say it's stupid.

"Clearly," I informed Dayton's publicity people, "the machine is schizophrenic and in some circumstances could be considered dangerous. To reinforce our faith, Dayton's simply is going to have to submit one of its executives to the machine. One would be disappointed to learn the Daytons are unwilling to accept the same hazards as their customers."

"Clearly," he said nervously, "one would."

And so the graph of the company vice-president's card here tells me, not surprisingly, that he is reliable, sincere, self-composed, has extraordinary ability, sometimes enjoys being alone, is attractive to the opposite sex, and is migratory — a mysterious category which makes one wonder whether George needs an escalator or a navigator.

In addition the machine credits George with an over-developed imagination, and this one alarms me faintly. The question is: Do I want a man with an over-developed imagination sending me bills at the end of each month?

The other question is: Did George pay the 75 cents in cash to the Anavac operator or did he use a charge-a-plate?

A Diplomatic Dolly from Trafalgar

Since the sunrise of U.S. history, Americans have been getting outmaneuvered, sandbagged, and routinely faked-out by English diplomats. This began when George III talked the colonies into taking Baltimore as a bonus in the treaty of independence.

I do not know why I should be surprised today, therefore, to discover I have been shrewdly finessed by a strawberry-haired young Englishwoman, who has manipulated me into the role of a dating agency. I think you are entitled to view the process as a case study in drygulchery.

My only intention was to grant Miss Peggy Salmon a public forum from which she could defend English cooking — an enterprise that requires not only a public forum but a good deal of imagination and in some cases an act of God.

Like most wrongheaded women, Miss Salmon stimulated me and aroused my compassion. In harmony with most of the men around here, I find misguided women to be harmless, generally. The exceptions here are the ones driving Crosstown 62, in which case they take on the hazardous qualities of a sputtering bomb.

If you have not traveled there, you should understand that the English — for all of their hundreds of admirable qualities — have been struggling for centuries to catch up with the mysteries of the kitchen and so far as I know are still trailing.

Miss Salmon called from her secretary's desk at Northrup King to request equal time for a counterattack. I agreed, and in the interest of fairness, decided to surround her with the trappings of English pubbery by taking a table in the beefeater-style restaurant of the Sheraton-Ritz.

I think the available bachelors in the audience today should be advised that Miss Salmon is lively, opinionated, attractive, in the age latitudes of 23 to 26, 5 feet 9 inches tall and acceptably filled out.

She sat there, however, regarding her calves' liver at the Sheraton-Ritz with a cool, gray neutrality. "The very best things about American food," she said, "are steak, apple pie and the Coney Island hot dogs sold by the A & W people."

She made this announcement evenly, with the kind of ageless English tact that blends charity with the long view of history.

"Beyond this, I do not understand what is this preoccupation you have with hamburger, in all of its works. Surely, there is more to life than chopped beef and fries. I think American roast beef, while it may have a lot of Worcestershire sauce, really does not have much character, and neither does most of the fish served here.

"The restaurants here are truly fine — Charlie's, Harry's and the Angus head my list — and in service and steaks American restaurants are unsurpassable by the English. But why do you smother the dinner with salads, why cannot you make tea, are there no other biscuits except chocolate chip and sugar cookies and cannot they serve simple breakfast pancakes at the restaurants here without overturning the fruit stand on them?"

Miss Salmon's eyes burned momentarily with the fervor of a Hyde Park orator. She now relaxed and apologized. "But I really have liked it very much here in the year I have been over — the baseball, bowling, outings, the lakes. I regret I am going to have to return to London. It's nothing specific. The men are very chivalrous but perhaps not overly aggressive.

"Bars like Duff's are a pretty good place to meet them, but you would have to say meetings such as these might lack, well, permanence. Clubs like Never on Friday are erratic. Outings are okay. I'm told, for example, that to beat the Minnesota winter all you have to do is buy a pair of downhills, a set of skis, and you're made."

"I believe the expression is," I said gently, " 'you've got it made.' "

"You use your expressions," Miss Salmon replied gently, "and I'll use mine."

There is no stubbornness, of course, like English stubbornness. I have to conclude Miss Salmon could be persuaded to stay, with the proper incentive. "On the chance there may be some curious Coney Island snackers in the audience," I inquired, "where might you be reachable?"

"I thought," she said, "you would never ask. My phone is 339-3526."

The Cool Red Tunnels Are Quiet

The red-earthed catacombs that have been burrowed a thousand feet under my home town by generations of helmeted miners are silent today, and soon will be sealed forever.

I trust there was no formal observance of the closing of the last underground iron ore mine in Ely. The Iron Range never did produce a trumpeter who could play Auld Lang Syne in four languages.

Beyond this, the only functions certain to draw crowds on the Range are Yugoslav picnics, come-as-you-are Finnish steam baths and the appearance of a random faith healer from Duluth.

Of the half-dozen underground mines that spilled millions of dollars worth of ore into the country's blast furnaces for more than a half-century, the remnants in Ely now are empty tunnels, dead earth.

The town will survive, partly because the underground's successor — the taconite industry — is operating nearby, and partly because the lakes and forests have outlasted the steam shovels, and the tourist will be there when the iron miner is gone.

And so the red-smudged skeleton of the abandoned mining shaft is not the town's headstone as it might have been years ago, before the years of social security, mining company pensions, unionization.

But while there may be future mining in the river-seamed hills near the town, the vermilion treasure that helped mechanize the nation has vanished.

With it, I'm sure, must go part of the community's personality. Until diluted by a stubbornly advancing civilization decades ago, it was the miniaturization of the brawling frontier; peopled by lumberjacks, miners and wenches.

But later the grime of its tunnels and the babel of its old world languages congealed into some tough-fibered essence of the American vision. The Industrialists had their millions from its vaults, and the immigrants had their dignity and the future of their children.

It may be well to remember that in a period of screaming protestors and whining beatniks there are still people around to whom the language at the foot of the Statue of Liberty was and is more than a parody.

And so an immigrant who arrived at Ellis Island 60 years ago with his name flapping from his lapel for the inspectors and fright in his eyes could live to see his son earning a rich man's salary as a scholarly researcher in space age electronics.

The era of the underground iron mine ends in northern Minnesota with no grievous enmity between the companies and the workers. There were walkouts, shutdowns and politicking but no enduring hatreds. The mining companies, exploiters once in the fashion of the times, later had no stomach for it and finally no opportunity for it.

They matured, as the pick-swinging miner did, and today they are spending millions, where they are not required to, to provide for and resettle the men who raised the earth.

For the men, the mines were a culture and a condition of life by themselves. They were their banks, their town halls, their prisons — because there was nothing else for them — and for a few of them, their graves.

Nobody had any secrets in those moist, cool ore drifts, where the minister's Sunday sermon underwent a blunt and enthusiastic critique each week.

There were very few pretensions. You got along in whatever language was convenient. I knew an Italian grocer who listened to 6 a.m. mass in Slovenian, ordered his beer in Finnish and for all I know romanced in Swahili.

The ore stockpiles were the playgrounds of the kids, their ski-slopes in the winter and their Badlands for cowboys-and-crooks in the summer. People around town knew what the 15th level was producing at the Zenith mine, and they knew what the emergency siren meant in the middle of the afternoon.

The idea of a college education for the children was an obsession with many of them and the reason they resisted when the son would plan to go underground to help raise money for it.

"Once you go down there," they would say, "you will never get out."

But many did, of course. And yet as the symbol of the youngster's arrival to manhood in this mining community — whatever he planned to do in the future — there was nothing with quite the emotional jar of the day he strapped on a helmet and battery and descended into the cool red tunnels with his father.

Some of the ghosts in the town are not sad ones.

The Visitor Forgot His Pants

He came weaving unevenly through the jail cell gate, steered by an embattled policeman who was trying to prevent him from capsizing.

His face had the scenically splotchy tones of a drunken sunset, from which wafted the determined scent of stale Virginia Dare.

He was wearing a white undershirt, striped shorts and the harried look of a man who has just made a hasty exit from some unidentified boudoir.

Incumbents in the overnight detention cell of the Minneapolis city jail could only speculate on what urgent chain of events impelled this luckless man into the cold night.

"He was found," explained the jailer, responding to our inquiring gazes, "in an abandoned snow bank, barely conscious and in need of guidance. We found this gray coat for him and, as soon as he sobers up and gives us his address, we should be able to find his pants."

Anonymously, the new enrollee was propped up on the floor in an irregular bunch, and the night droned on apace in the aromatic community cell known sentimentally among its alumni as "the tank."

I observed this affecting little vignette as an amateur and undercover jailbird under a visa authorized informally by the courthouse management, which allowed me behind-bars privileges for the purpose of gathering research material.

We will explore "the tank" at a later time, but I thought you ought to know there are free-wheeling enterprisers there who may yet go far in the investment business.

One of them, a curly-haired 23-year-old with bright eyes and a fondness for bum checks, asked me for the loan of a dime to make a call from the pay phone adjacent to the tank.

"It's the only dime I have," I said.

"You'll get it back," he countered. "I'll make the call, but you'll get your money back, I guarantee you."

Intrigued, I released the dime. The check artist obtained permission to make the call and was back in five minutes.

"You made the call?" I asked. He nodded. "But it didn't cost me a thing, and if you'll stop looking goggle-eyed I'll tell you why.

"The telephone company makes dividends on squares like you. All you do, dial the operator. She answers and you get the dime back you just put in, right? Okay, then you tell her you dialed a number but it was busy, and that you didn't get your dime back. So you ask her to dial the number for you, and she co-operates very politely."

I was going to say "astounding," but remembered my incognito in time and settled for "crazy, man."

"Well, it ain't much of a dodge," he said, "but it ain't bad under the conditions."

My floormate on the right, an unclassified lush from Kentucky, monitored the conversation unimpressed. He spoke in a split-octave voice from which most of the raspiness had been lubricated away by a quart of gin that may have been cheap but at least was lousy.

"Five hours," he mourned under his wooled bill cap. "Five hours I'm out on the street and they bring me back in."

"A guy," I said, "ought to have a little more will power than that."

"Will power got nuthin' to do with it," he said. "With me, it was a fight. I just didn't like the looks of this other guy when they were loading up the patrol wagon. I'll get six months sure."

"For a fight?" I asked, puzzled.

"The other man," the hillbilly said sadly, "was wearin' a blue coat and a big brass button."

A Little Girl's Last Train Ride

Her fingernails were gaily polished red, her checked dress freshly pressed. In her hair was the blue clasp she wore to birthday parties.

She was cradled in her mother's lap on the observation car of the Milwaukee Road's Hiawatha, a tidy young lady.

A dying little girl, taking her last train ride.

She had been on a train two years before and remembered the excitement of its speed, the trees and houses racing by her window, the thumping underneath her.

She had laughed and squealed then but today her face was frozen into partial paralysis, the stamp of a brain tumor that will take Terri Ann Duskin's life within weeks. Perhaps tomorrow. Perhaps tonight.

A week before she had been taken to the animal farm at Brookdale and a day later to the Easter display at Montgomery Ward's in Robbinsdale because her parents wished to give her what she would most enjoy in these final days of her life.

A porter lifted her tenderly from her wheel chair and carried her into the observation car for the 25-minute ride from Minneapolis to St. Paul.

She lay limply in the arms of her mother, Mrs. Harry Duskin, wordless and impassive – not in her heart and mind, for she can still reason and remember and feel.

But the spreading suffocation of the brain growth has robbed her of the power to express herself with her lips and eyes.

Except that as the train began to glide out of the station the left side of her face formed the wan, crooked travesty of a smile and her mother tightened her own hand around the girl's.

Industrial plants and decaying houses raced past along the route. To scores of vacationing children in the forward cars and the domed cruiser, they were castles, forts and skyscrapers.

To Mrs. Harry Duskin they were ashes.

But what were they to the 5-year-old girl who now raised an arm weakly to wave at an automobile?

"Don't you want to get up and look?" the mother asked.

The child did not respond but rested her head on the mother's shoulder. The mother was smiling and teasing and the little girl did not know there was no heart in the gaiety or that when her mother turned her head it was to weep.

Vacantly the mother looked out the window on the opposite side of the car. Until a year ago Terri Ann was healthy and active, fond of playing house, wearing her mother's hats.

She began falling down stairs, groping in places with which she should have been easily familiar. She was taken to hospitals. There were treatments and diagnosis. In January she lost her power of speech, could form only the word "momma."

A short time ago, doctors told the father, a restaurant employe, the child probably would not reach her sixth birthday, three months from now. There was no hope in surgery, although treatments might prolong her life.

The girl was brought home, re-united with her parents, her brother and sisters, and the two foster children whom the young couple had adopted several years ago.

The mother, a dark-haired, attractive woman of 26, accepted the medical estimate – and yet she did not.

"I am like any other mother," she said. "I can't bring myself to give up hope. But I can see what is happening to the girl. I don't want to think ahead. All we're doing is to try to make her happy, and even if she doesn't show it, I know she is."

At their home Sunday at 6014 North Fremont they had their Easter dinner a week early. The girl found her basket near her bed, where she would not have to grope for it.

On the train with her and her mother Thursday were Todd, Linda Dahl and her grandmother, Rose Gaynor.

"She slipped into a coma over the weekend," Mrs. Gaynor said, "and we thought she would not wake up, because one of the doctors said it probably would come this way. But she did, and she seemed cheerful again. But today she doesn't have much spirit any more."

Todd, the brother, was kneeling on the car seat and clutching the window frame, babbling breathlessly in the fashion of a 4-year-old boy on a train. A conductor walked in and pinned a Hiawatha button on the girl's dress, but she did not respond, and he understood.

The train eased along the river and slid into the St. Paul station, where a porter carried the girl into the big toy-train-yard off the main lobby. For a few minutes she watched the little trains bustling in the sand, and then she was placed in her wheelchair.

Her father drove up to the station in the family car and they went back to Minneapolis.

The girl seemed tired and drowsy. The hospital identification band on her wrist touched her eyes as she placed her head on her mother's shoulder.

"I know she enjoyed the train ride," her mother said.

(Four months later, the little girl died.)

Game Ball to St. Peter

Now that the Green Bay Packers have routed the Chiefs, the Colts, the Bears and the Lions, all that is left is for someone to bring on the Christians.

In its stumbling but steadfast fashion, the nation survived Super Sunday, thus vindicating the simple faith of the founding fathers who predicted this land would have to endure hours of agonizing national trial – such as epidemics, wars, depressions, and Nielsen ratings – to demonstrate its greatness.

And somehow one feels today, with our constancy tested anew, shaken but still unbroken, that we are going to be all right now in Vietnam and in the 1967 Minnesota Legislature.

For all of this bounty, I say we owe a moral debt to the Green Bay Packers and Vince Lombardi, the one fixed star of sanity in TV football's otherwise deranged universe.

Lombardi, of course, swept most of the day's artistic honors, outglowing such strong competition as Ray Scott, Curt Gowdy, Paul Christman, Bart Starr, Max McGee and the driver of the ski-jumping Ford automobile in the commercial.

Vince stood there in shirt sleeves in the post-game dressing room, tolerating the quaking scribes around him. Lombardi does not conduct interviews so much as he grants audiences. His are the only press conferences in the NFL where the questioner not only raises his hand but removes his hat.

Vinnie was brandishing the game ball and wearing that befuddling smile which seemed to suggest to the timid inquisition around him: "All right, shall we answer all of your stupid questions individually or shall we take them collectively?"

The average reporter never knows quite how to react when Vince smiles at him, whether to feel anointed or to start worrying in the fashion of a man who has just been flattered unexpectedly by the neighborhood undertaker.

Strictly as a mopping-up exercise, however, it was pretty fair theater, surpassing in spontaneity and suspense the football game that preceded it.

The Chiefs must have had a presentiment of what was coming when, en route to his halftime meeting with the squad, Lombardi bypassed the usual formalities and instead of opening the dressing room door simply walked through it.

You may have noticed that the Chiefs appeared jarred and

unsteady to open the second half. This was because they had to pass the Packer locker room on their way back to the field. They were expecting the scent of liniment. Somebody forgot to tell them Lombardi uses incense and sulphur.

In any case, the Packers, who had played the first half using the sleepwalker's shift, routinely demolished the Chiefs in the second half and thus cleared the way for the second annual Super Bowl, which next year will be played on Mars.

Moving the game into the heavens would tend, unfortunately, to give the homefield advantage to Lombardi.

For all of its excessive ardor in the pre-game promotion, I thought television generally delivered a rather competent and tasteful performance considering the absence of dramatic putty to work with. Outstanding in this area, of course, was one of the sponsors, the Ford Motor Company, which demonstrated the ability of its automobiles to leap down ski slopes and ride the rapids.

"All of that encourages me," one of the neighboring oglers said. "I'm glad to know my Ford can ski and run down the cascades. Now I wonder if it would be asking too much to get the damn thing to start in the morning."

For pure entertainment, though, nothing I saw the last three hours upstaged your friend and mine, Norman Van Brocklin, who, in describing the splay-footed running style of Kansas City's Mike Garrett, decided that "the guy runs like ten minutes to two."

Dutch, of course, wrought another one of his more modest off-season miracles by appearing taped on two channels simultaneously in the pre-game. The man clearly is beyond reach not only of the NFL but also the Federal Communication Commission and the laws of gravity.

And yet, the Dutchman seemed lonely, sitting there at the table without Rollie Johnson.

So did the Chiefs, sitting there 25 points behind, with no commercials left. They might have spared themselves the travail by heeding the advice of Johnny Unitas. They asked Unitas in the pre-game what is the best strategy against the Packers. "The best thing to do," Unitas concluded, "is give up."

Policemen's Brawl

In the timeless struggle on the city streets between the police and prostitutes, we discover with some dismay today that the prostitutes are now leading by percentage points.

This dramatic flip-flop in the race as it heads past mid-September is occasioned by events of the last 24 hours in city hall, where there is a serious question as to which group has more people under investigation, the criminals or the captains.

The essential facts are these: Captain Eugene Wilson, an officer with a commendable record but an incendiary disposition, has been suspended for writing a memo dealing with the allegedly high incidence of prostitution, pimping, gambling and drug-pushing in his downtown precinct.

Wilson used to command the city vice squad, which, with our peculiar passion for positive thinking, we have re-named the morals squad. His superiors have concluded that the captain, in his latest plunge into authorship, is simply playing politics again. I do not expect Wilson to acknowledge this. But if he did, I suspect his defense would consist of the point that he is hardly being original playing politics on the police force, where it is not a game but a condition of employment.

To defend himself, Wilson has obtained a court order that has the effect of suspending the suspension. We will now await the hearing in a state of high civic tension. None of us can pre-judge the merit of the accusations brought against the captain. We are aware in a general way of the exasperation of police chief Hawkinson — who is charging Wilson with insubordination, dereliction, insincerity and, for all I know, halitosis at the policeman's ball.

Purely as a problem of police discipline, Captain Wilson admittedly has been an administrative Mexican jumping bean the past two years, in that he has been lively, mobile and unforecastable. Curiously, his troubles did begin in Acapulco — which, again, does not make him original.

But the latest wrangle among the hawkshaws puts the public in the novel position of needing a squad room roster to tell which cop is in court as a witness nowadays and which one is there as a defendant. It also focuses attention anew on the migratory habits of the city's prostitutes, a matter to which even the most conservative readers should address themselves.

The question is: Where are they now?

The captain maintains they are still around the core city in force, and we shall have to see what corroborating evidence he produces. You will recall the center for this sort of activity used to be Washington Avenue. But, like the Metropolitan Building and the Bijou Theater, it gave way to the urban renewer's maul; and what was once a seraglio is now a parking lot.

From there the salesgirls moved to 6th and Hennepin. But, after flourishing there for several years, they were forced into general retreat by tougher ordinances and the high gallantry of the police — who risked a hammering on the head now and then by the spiked heels of the more combative girls and as a result were made eligible for Boulevard Battle Stars.

The underlying reason why prostitution waned on 6th and Hennepin, however, may have been more subtle. With the playboys adopting new hair styles, it became increasingly difficult for potential customers to tell the difference between the harlots and the hippies.

And so some then moved — and this, of course, was an integrated process — into North Minneapolis, where they have needed Molotov cocktails to do business from time to time. The activity may now center around Nicollet and Grant. But there is hope there, too, because the freeways are about to go in near there and, as a practical matter, it is tough to hustle in a sandpit.

Which leaves uncertain the fate of an extremely interesting proposal by the Star's editorial page scholars, that women police officers be used to put the arm on would-be clients who propositioned them.

I do not doubt the city police force women's division has dedicated officers who could handle this type of patrol. But you must see the pitfall immediately. A shapely policewoman loiters on the corner and is approached by a man with a blue blazer and a furtive look.

"You," the policewoman says, after the predictable negotiation, "are under arrest."

"You can't arrest me," the man replies. "I'm Hobbs, of the morals squad, working undercover."

With no alternative, they arrest each other and exit together, handcuffed fraternally.

Fight Fiercely, Fat Girls

Years of sympathetic scrutiny have convinced me there is no such thing as a bad fat woman.

Bad advice, bad diets and bad girdle snaps, yes. But I will ask the men among us, how many times have you been betrayed by an overweight blonde or falsely tempted by a blimpy brunette?

No, I think we have no argument about their loyalty to their men. All that remains now is for somebody to get their noses out of the ice cream dish and their fingers out of the bonbons.

In this, I think it's fair to note, the doctors largely have failed. I say this despite a cloudburst of telephone calls from women asking me to identify the doctor who hypnotized a middle-aged switchboard operator into the loss of 62 pounds.

I do not know the doctor's name, nor the psychic mysteries of the particular woman who convinced herself the hypnosis was working. To those who have asked me to intervene for them, I can only note that (a) dieting is too serious a matter to be entrusted to doctors under normal circumstances and (b) I think I can reduce you by 10 pounds within two or three weeks if you agree to stop coddling yourselves and quit chasing pills, injections, sorcerers, trances and dietetic candy.

My reservation about accepting medical advice on dieting is that most doctors, well-intentioned and considerate, of course, are not tough enough with their patients. My own doctor urged me not to abandon cigarettes at a time when I was launching a campaign to remove 50 pounds in three months. He contended the net effect of all this deprivation might be too much for the nervous system and might send me careening off into some kind of psychological oblivion.

This prospect seemed agreeable to the Star's city editor, Lee Canning, to whom hysteria is familiar since it is part of the specifications of his job. Canning suggested I go full throttle on the diet, no cigarettes and all. I may have told you after four weeks the doctor, who had a small weight problem of his own, was calling **me** for advice. After six weeks he joined the YMCA, has lost 20 pounds, and is doing very well.

And thus you should be counseled that doctors really aren't soliciting diet business. Beyond this, I suspect that the most lasting hypnotic relationship between doctor and patient lies in the simple act of presenting the bill, which in some cases will leave you positively paralyzed.

"The trouble with a lot of dieters," a medical confidante told me, "is that they're looking for some kind of crutch. They may go for fads, goofy diets, quacks. There is nothing much any tough-minded doctor can tell you except to get the hell away from the cookie jar."

Which, lady, is what I am telling you. And now because we are good and trusting friends, I am offering to do your accounting in the belief you need a rooting section. If you do not believe you can discipline yourself, however, turn immediately to Dear Abby.

Buy a calorie counter and literally count your calories. For breakfast have a half of unsweetened grapefruit, a couple of wafers of melba toast, coffee or tea. For lunch broiled ground round and cottage cheese and lettuce salad with wine vinegar. For dinner, lean meat, a small fruit plate, lettuce salad. Eat all of the raw vegetables and greens you want. Hold your caloric intake to about 1,300 a day and get out and walk around the neighborhood or otherwise exercise.

I'm not interested in your objections. If you don't want it this way, take your troubles to Fanny Farmer. For these three weeks you will take no potatoes, bread, butter, pie, cake, candy, cocktails or beer (unless you spend a weekend in Munich, when you are forgiven a liter of Lowenbrau).

Because the hour between 9 and 10 a.m. on Mondays is one during which I need an outward display of activity to keep Canning away from my desk, I will accept your weekly weight report in the mail on that day. You do not have to identify yourself and may even resort to cryptology, such as "Agent 187 from Orono."

And now, on the chance that a little hypnosis truly might soothe you at the outset, your lids are growing heavy, you have a warm, comfortable sensation, your cares are receding, reced ---zzzzzzzz.

(Note: Mr. Klobuchar has fallen asleep, but will reply to your mail on receipt.)

Look Out! It's Freeway Florence

In its long march toward salvation, mankind has learned to live with the woman driver – not as a hazard to be outwitted but as a natural calamity to be outlasted.

I raise the point today because I have just discovered the living and breathing embodiment of the institution we have come to love and occasionally fear. Florence is the hostess at Nye's Polonaise, a popular chophouse and sauerkraut foundry on E. Hennepin. She is known for her clothes, loveliness, flaky conversation and looping left turns.

"Everybody," she disclosed, "complains about the traffic around here and about how complicated the freeway interchanges are. I used to be confused, too, until I reasoned it out. Now, all I do is use a simple rule. When I want to go left, I take the second turn to the right."

Alarmed, I rushed to Bob Provost, who is my personal consultant in the field of auto safety. As spokesman for the Insurance Information Center, Provost is paid to tell us why we should be grateful that auto insurance rates are not higher. He is also one of the world's great and understanding authorities on the subject of women drivers.

"Florence," Provost explained, "is probably typical of many women drivers in that she appears to drive intuitively."

"I would be content," I interrupted, "if she simply drove predictably."

"No, what I mean is that, driving in this manner, she is probably right most of the time. And undoubtedly she is right more often than men who depend purely on the highway signs to point them in the right direction on, let us say, Hwys. 35W and crosstown 62 south of Minneapolis. My advice, therefore, to a driver following Florence is to drive with respect, humility, and a wary hand on the wheel," Provost said.

"By a twist of coincidence, I have just returned from southern Minnesota, where I did some research on this subject. One of the great charms of women drivers is the absence of any forecastable pattern in how they will perform. Some, from whom you would not expect it, are beautiful drivers. On the other hand, near Faribault I was passed by a nun who was driving 30 miles an hour over the speed limit."

"Undoubtedly," I observed, "this is one of the dangers of

mixing piety with sobriety. Why didn't you counsel with her at the next stop?"

"There are dangers in this, too," Provost explained. "I know a traffic expert in a small town who did this very thing. The driver turned out to be a priest. My friend thus became the only Catholic in town who had to ask for a change in venue when he went to confession."

No man of any wisdom or prudence, of course, is going to put the knock on women drivers in any broad generalization. I'm sure you know that women drivers are uniformly better insurance risks than men, that they drive more cautiously, they drink less, they drive less in bad weather, and are seldom preoccupied with blondes in the front seat.

"And yet two things stand out as obstacles to driving proficiency among women," Provost observed. "One is that most of them follow too closely, which some psychologists may ascribe to a kind of apron-string school of driving but which may simply be the result of dirty windshields. Also, they do not back up very well – a trait that often can lead them into embarrassing situations such as hedges and garage doors.

"Their one big plus, however, is the absence of any driving conceit. With most men, driving prowess stands among the top three symbols of masculine vanity, the other two being their ability to ring the bell at the carnival midway and to do more or less the same thing in the boudoir.

"To those women who are earnestly interested in becoming good drivers, I would say take lessons from professionals. Don't be instructed by your husband, which is bad; or your boy friend, which is worse. Above everything, women should try to avoid emotional distractions while driving.

"I can think of no more perilous situation, for example, than that posed by a dedicated housewife, running 30 minutes late, worried about her hair, heading for the weekly social and wondering whether she will be the last one there."

"But wouldn't it depend partly on which of the family automobiles she was driving?" I asked loyally.

"If you mean is there such a thing as a kind of optimum, ideal vehicle to match a lady's driving habits," Provost said, "I cannot think of any, unless it might be a Jefferson bus."

The Little Eden Across the Creek

NOTE: Concluding his unauthorized tour of Minneapolis suburbia, the writer herein guides you through the scenic paths and the fetching gingerbread homes of the village of Edina. It is one of the few places in the country where millionaires, civic angels and athletic prodigies co-exist peacefully. Jocularly, the columnist also maintains it is the only suburb requiring a temporary visa for entry.

EDINA, Minnesota – Welcome to Camelot.

Yes, some of its castles are mortgaged; but surely there is no more congenial spot for civic galahading, for happy cocktail houring and for a fraternal bliss which once more confirms the old adage: It is possible to have money and still enjoy life.

This is a community so Utopian it has become a fairytale caricature, a never-never land of metropolitan society in which its athletic plumed knights almost never lose; where good fortune and civic rectitude abound; where the average family income is the fourth highest in the nation ($5 ahead of Hollywood's Beverly Hills); where, in the fashion of a Gilbert and Sullivan chorus the natives sing that nothing could be better or fairer and where even enemies – such as the school superintendent and village manager – speak well of each other.

In the face of all this virtue, wealth, good works and athletic perfection, the stranger has his choice either of running to Bloomington, where there is a smattering of sin and at least a suggestion of mortality here and there to leaven the atmosphere, or stopping at Clancy's Drug in Edina for a cool glass of Fresca to survey this man-made miracle with some degree of calm perspective.

The visitor may be impressed that, among other things, Edina is a good deal larger than a year ago. While neighboring Bloomington produces a storm of publicity releases about its growth, for example, with understandable pride, it was Edina which recorded the largest growth from the spring of 1966 to the spring of 1967 – some 3,500 up to approximately 40,000.

Not all of the new Edinans are millionaires. Some are the children of millionaires and a few are good, ambitious, plugging latter-day country clubbers whose fathers left them the business and their credit cards.

In addition, Edina has now fully annexed the neighboring community of Morningside, an amalgamation which in a rather extraordinary way evoked claims of defeat from both sides.

To the motoring visitor, the homes may have an esthetic spread ranging from grand to wondrous to expensively vulgar. You will encounter a few where the architectural rock has been so casually and aimlessly distributed as to leave the viewer in doubt about whether this is a house or a quarry.

But there is a pervading good taste and discrimination, largely the community's legacy — the natives tell me — from a Scandinavian builder named Carl Hansen, who arrived in the country with a hammer and rusty nail and wrought much of the extravaganza that is Edina today.

It was a place to which the wealthy naturally gravitated, outside of the turbulence and aromas of the core city and into an environment of repose in which the residents could enjoy their mutual good fortune without being routed in the 5 o'clock rush or being interred by a falling warehouse.

And so the well-to-do accumulated here in a setting of truly exceptional natural beauty and becoming exclusivity. Only Shaker Heights outside of Cleveland, Ohio, and two Chicago suburbs have an average family income higher than Edina's $12,000 plus, and the competitive dwellers here apparently have decided to make it a contest.

Among metropolitan suburbs less favored by providence and the stock exchange, Edina's snobbery has become proverbial. Undoubtedly it is overstated by the envious and the malevolent. In some neighborhoods, true, there is a rather neurotic and feverish race to stay at least even with the people next door and, it is hoped, pass them on the nearest turn. This can lead to personality quirks of many descriptions, including a deliberate risk of bankruptcy.

Thus one does not need millions to live in Edina as much as he needs a patient banker.

By far, however, most of the townspeople belong here and are giddily glad to be here.

But they have a reasonable amount of intramural strife, for all of the serenity in the residential areas and in the energetic shopping district known as 50th and France.

For one thing, the village manager (who draws about $21,000) figures the school superintendent (who draws about $27,000) is overpaid in relation to what other high village officials get — namely the village manager.

Further, the manager is not quite sure he understands why the school superintendent should need a public relations counsel, recently appointed, to communicate with the school staff and the public.

Edina wins in football, basketball, hockey, and various other pursuits in the Lake Conference and probably would win in the Big Ten if it expanded its recruiting beyond the present level. It wins, of course, mostly with homegrowns and is no more aggressive in outside recruiting than its Lake Conference rivals. It is merely more successful.

No high school athletic teams around have firmer discipline, or uniformly better coaching, or more genuine encouragement from the parents or the student body.

This may be an anomaly in a ritzy atmosphere in which the kids compete, but it is simply a fact.

One can only marvel at the consequences if the village had access to the bulk of the tax revenue flowing out of the world's largest general store, Southdale.

It is difficult to imagine, however, what Edina would do with more money, although it is open to speculation.

Southdale is not unanimously popular with the natives and there are continuing and strong loyalties to the tidy and accommodating district near 50th and France where you may buy:

Bagels at the Edina Kitchen, first-rate sausage at Hackenmuellers, limitless produce at Lund's and National, and practically anything else at Clancy's Drug.

The service here is excellent, the courtesy genuine. Regrettably, the village could use a first-rate restaurant but draws $300,000 from the municipal liquor store and has no galloping need for private liquor with Bloomington so close by.

And who would want to change this sociable little hamlet, after all? It could go into foreign aid, but why bother. Onc gathers Edina is content to keep what it has, including the local franchise to cash the credit cards from Monte Carlo.

The Sporting Set Convenes at Stillwater

They put the Twins' Billy Martin behind bars for two hours with 200 inmates of Stillwater Prison Friday night. The encounter ended predictably. Martin, a long-term talker, finished with a suspended sentence.

"I have come here," Martin explained to an inquisitive turnkey in advance of the prison's annual athletic awards banquet, "in response to numerous requests from such people as Howie Fox, Johnny Sain, Jim Kaat and my wife—who figured it might be a good idea to scout the joint in case my lawyer has an off day when they try that $100,000 suit."

Martin is the Twins' coach who speaks a kind of antipasto English leavened by jittery body movements, the occupational hazard of a man who relays signs at third base. Where another man might putter with his tie or play with his watch in public, Martin thrashes around like a worried dervish, slapping his face and clutching his shirt front at odd moments as though somebody let the flies in.

He spent ten minutes explaining to the inmates the intricacies of the Twins' supersecret signal system of signs and countersigns. "Fine, Martin," said an appreciative burglar at my table. "Now I wonder if it would be asking too much to perform the same service for the Twins' baserunners?"

"We look for a big year," Martin continued, unruffled, "from Earl Battey who, when I last saw him, was 220 pounds and paying his taxes – the best news of the winter for the club and the federal government."

Martin, of course, is richly cherished by inmate audiences. They see in him a type of kindred soul whose violent impulses, fortunately, were steered into beneficial channels through his early associations with such redemptive characters as Hank Bauer, Mickey Mantle and Yogi Berra.

"Coach Martin," an inmate asked in the post-banquet cross-examination. "There's one thing a lot of us around here have been curious about. Is your nose really that big or have you got a short visor on your baseball cap?"

This so unhinged the coach as to prompt him to summon relief, which materialized in the form of announcer Ray Scott. Scott was preoccupied with football and his Green Bay chum, Vince Lombardi. It was the first time I have ever heard a football coach quoted in the invocation, although I have heard Rollie Johnson come close on Channel 4.

It was one of the more memorable evenings of the season, however, enhanced by the sight of a district judge, Gene Minenko, distributing his professional card to inmate diners at our table.

"You got any graduates from your courtroom in here, judge?" an inmate wanted to know.

"Everybody has off days," Minenko said. "The ones I'm worried about are some of my old clients from the days when I was a defense attorney. When a judge makes a mistake he gets overruled. When an attorney makes a mistake, the client gets two years."

The warden, Ralph Tahash, presided over the presentation of awards for athletic excellence to deserving inmates. Regrettably, he was unable to honor one of the athletes of the year, who had trained himself to a fine edge and vented his competitive urges on the head of an arguing cellmate. He was given the award in absentia.

"The guy may be spending time in the hole," grumbled the inmate football coach, Dub Dunleavy, "but at least he gets something. Me, I had an up-and-down year with my ball club. But we ain't losing anybody next year and we got at least three or four hotshot transfers coming in from the St. Cloud Reformatory, I understand.

"We have nothing but good reports on these boys."

Dunleavy is one of the irresistible characters in the institution, a mingling of the finer qualities of Knute Rockne, Jackie Gleason and Jesse James.

"I used to admire credit cards," he explained. "So much so that I tried makin' a few myself.

"But about my ball club, we got help in midseason, you remember, from this fullback I used to coach at the Fort Madison Penitentiary in Iowa. We sort of followed each other up to Stillwater. There are a lot of things you appreciate in this world, but I mean loyalty goes right there at the top of the list. However, we are still a little thin at some positions."

The judge regarded a chicken leg in his right hand. "Let me know what you need, coach," the judge observed. "I'll see what I can do."

An Old Tailor Named Noodleman

He was blubbering and smiling; it was hard to distinguish which. He wore an oversize hospital robe, white sweat socks and high-backed leather slippers of an old vintage that suggested a curled toe and an impending squeak.

Three weeks ago he was nearly dead. Now he was shuffling about the corridors restlessly, only 15 per cent of his stomach left but with all his consonants and vowels out of place as usual.

He was an old tailor who seemed to belong in a world of gingerbread men and spinning wheels, candy canes and plump shoemakers.

A wisp of white hair rimmed his bald head and gave him the droll appearance of an animated figure romping about the cartoonist's drawing board, bent on good works but prone to fumble.

A funny old man, P. Noodleman the Tailor, but I think a pretty important piece of humanity for all that, an obscure little man touched by a stubborn and baggy-pants nobility.

They feared for his life when they took him to the hospital and discovered a tumor that had to be removed. It was, and within a week Noodleman was sizing patients across the hall, speculating on the amount of cloth to shear from the garment to make it wearable.

His scrambled speech and gentle admonitions convulsed the nurses at Mount Sinai Hospital, but he started getting footloose this week. Friday the hospital released him and said it was all right to reopen his shop in two weeks, thus relieving the anxieties of customers who had darkly contemplated a winter of sagging drawers.

His workshop at 7th and Portland in the Sexton Building has been there for decades, and so have his 50-year-old steam iron and foot-pedal Singer sewer.

I do not know whether, at 74, his self-authorized age, Noodleman retains all his old craftsmanship. I don't think it really matters, and I have grounds to suspect that his modest prices and Goldwynesque language appeal to customers at least as much as his old immigrant skills.

Blissfully, the little rascal scoffs at rulings from the customhouse tailors —that a man losing X number of pounds simply cannot be retailored.

His methods horrify new-schoolers among the tailors. His daughter, Mrs. George Black, with whom he lives, suggested that I remove two of my suits from his racks three weeks ago when it appeared that the tailor would be hospitalized for months.

I shopped these white-threaded shreds around Minneapolis for a week before getting a taker in Northfield, Minnesota, who contended that trying to pick up in midstream from Noodleman was like trying to break the CIA code.

Absent-minded, he has been known to lose a pair of pants (mine) between the pages of a two-year-old calendar hanging from some forgotten back wall. For all this, he dreads misplacing clothes and once, fearing that a customer had taken the wrong trousers, dashed eight blocks into an office building. "Have you seen a pair of pants come through here?" he asked the elevator operator urgently.

"Only those," the man replied, "with somebody in them."

True, his fingers have lost a little of their old dexterity and I will acknowledge that a month ago he not only pinned my coat cuff and shirt at a fitting but also lacerated my left arm and scored a near miss on the skin of my seat.

"Ah," he laughed at this, "once in a leetle while I get too close, no?" I asked whether he awards Purple Hearts, depending on the location of the wound, but Noodleman had run a tape measure around my neck now and had induced a pale purple glow from my cheeks.

Years ago he emerged as the unpublicized hero of one of the season's major society weddings by getting up at 2 a.m. to tailor a $300 suit for the father of the bride, working six hours nonstop while the agitated father plied him with coffee and threaded his needles.

But he is back home now and pining for a return to his shop, which for more than five decades has been his life, his solace and, apart from the synagogue, his sanctuary.

And so it seems to me that this old man, a Russian-born Jew, is as much a man for the season of tomorrow's Christmas as any I know. He is an amusing little fellow but graced by the dignity of his work. And, thankfully, he has not allowed himself the luxury of growing old calmly.

The Bicyclist's Sorry End

Among the instruments of prolonged torture I have just discovered a new entry to take its place beside dripping water, bamboo shoots under the fingernails, and three-hour baseball games.

I took a 100-mile Sunday drive yesterday — on a bicycle equipped with a hard leather seat of unexampled tyranny that inflicted stabbing pain and saddle sores in at least five places: Maple Plain, Hanover, St. Michael, Elk River, and Robbinsdale.

I don't know whether 100 miles by bicycle in Sunday traffic is a record around here or even a good average. Only the insurance companies know, and they don't talk unless they raise rates.

The only thing I know for certain is that I slept standing up last night, literally and uninterruptedly, and for the first time in my life drove my automobile into work this morning from a kneeling position.

The Minnesota chapter of the American Youth Hostelers euchered me into the bike ride, one of their spring projects. Very quickly it became a survival fight between the cyclists on one hand and their natural enemies, motorists and tall dogs, on the other.

8:30 a.m. — at Lake Calhoun: "A man," says Stan Bezanson, the expedition chief, "has to hate himself a little to take a 100-mile bike ride with the temperature below freezing and the wind up to 30 miles an hour."

We are riding those spare-framed, multiple-geared bikes with which the Europeans used to get around before they found out how to drive automobiles by using the horn. The seat is a tiny triangle without contours or compassion. It is like sitting on a bobbing flatiron for eight hours.

9:30 a.m. — a mile north of Wayzata: My gear shift lever breaks off, locking the gear in high against the wind and at the bottom of a half-mile hill. I am laboring and in great sweat and discomfort, and a Chrysler pulls abreast. The driver is lonesome and wants to socialize while we are riding in tandem. I give him a savage look and directions to the nearest freeway.

10:30 a.m. — at Maple Plain: We brunch at 22 miles and there are people among the 25 starters who discover they are needed at home in the afternoon. We leave with 15 riders, and for the next 10 miles I ride double-saddle with Bezanson. Animals become more aggressive as we near Loretto. I learn the cyclist's basic feinting maneuver when accosted by pursuing dogs.

There is a spaniel bearing down on the rider ahead of us, on a collision course. The dog has the angle on the rider, but just before the interception point the cyclist brakes suddenly. The spaniel, with momentum up, goes rolling down an embankment and into a reed-filled swamp. He rises and gives the cyclist the canine version of an indelicate gesture.

1 p.m. — at St. Michael: We are out some 47 miles now and are aswarm in the heady and mingling fragrances of the barnyard. At St. Michael, we stop for lunch. The town cafe is closed. There is a parish Sunday dinner at the school, but the lines stretch into the street. We dine on pretzels and coke at the dance hall in St. Michael. The Twins are on TV and the Tigers have the bases loaded with nobody out, which is about where I left them Friday night; so we head for Albertville.

4 p.m. — at the town of Nowthen, between Elk River and St. Francis: We are now down to eight riders and stop at the Jolly Hour tavern for snacks. "You bicycling 100 miles?" a farmer asks amiably. We nod. "What drunken navigator scheduled you to stop at Nowthen at 4 p.m.?" The farmer appraised us. "You need nourishment," he said. "Here, it ain't much, but have some of my potato chips." There was an unspoken bond here, the rural dweller offering sustenance to his distressed cousin from the city. "You from Minneapolis?" the farmer asked. We nodded. "When," he asked timelessly, "will they ever learn?"

6 p.m. — in Minneapolis: We have ridden through Anoka and are now sprinting along Highway 103 past the Starlite Theater. One of the club's automobiles is riding with us, picking up survivors. I am now riding in the upright position, even downhill. We swing past Cedar Lake and a motorist runs me into a ditch.

But it was one of those gripping experiences, and if you ask me would I do it all over again, I would tell you: Surely, you must be out of your mind.

To the Soldier With Blood on His Face

A squad leader in Vietnam writes, expressing some doubt as to which should worry him more — the Viet Congs, the violence in the United States or the five members of his squad who are on marijuana.

"Would you kindly tell me," he asks, "what in hell has happened to the America of the history books; why should I try to be so noble about spilling my guts over here while long-haired kwiffies get away with burning their draft cards; and why should I be a sucker and keep on doing it when I get chances to bug out?"

The only creditable advice on this, sergeant, is not to be unhinged by the sermonizers on the issues and motives of the Vietnam war. I appreciate, for example, that Dr. Judd may be in full possession of the accumulated truth of the centuries on the subject of the Far East, but there are times when being infallible simply is inadequate to meet the situation.

On the other side, Sen. McCarthy is often too distant and airy to be a believable leader among the people who want to end it now. You get the impression the senator is speaking for the Congressional Record and the Washington Post rather than the people who put him in office.

And so while the public here stumbles in confusion in the face of discord among such distinguished politicians as Judd and McCarthy, it is hard to see how the national purpose in Vietnam is going to be any more clear to a man with the carbine and the trenching tools and blood on his face.

I would not worry about the pot-consumers in your squad. They are outnumbered by some of the pot-consumers in the local algebra classes. These are the times, sergeant. Marijuana is taking on the kind of respectability that used to be reserved for Canadian Club and Hamm's Beer, and I suppose we may as well get used to it.

Most of us know no more than you what moral right we have to be in Vietnam or what political and military urgencies are keeping us there. In some fashion the country has bungled into inflating the war into a situation from which retreat seems impossible and advance seems impractical.

Nobody loses his faith in fairytales as quickly as a man

under mortar attack. I don't think you should be asked to fight the Vietnam war for the kid next door or your wife or girl friend or democracy or the administration.

Do it for yourself and the men who serve with you. In the miserable and melancholy war you have been asked to fight, nothing else really has much relevance. Sooner or later and in one form or another every man is examined for his toughness under stress. For the lucky ones it may be a fourth down and one in a football game or the wrong move at an office party. For some, crisis may never go deeper than that.

You have been thrown into a place where the personal crises come often, intimately and in a state of profound misery. You are probably going to come out of it, and you will remember how you faced it, and the men with whom you fought will remember. In the end, this may be all that you have to remember about Vietnam.

There is one other thing to remember. There are millions of people who do understand, that it is possible for them to be uncertain about our direction in Vietnam and still be heartsick and angered by the irony of a man getting shot at in a war that has divided his country and confused its people.

We might end it quickly, sergeant, but the country has neither the history nor the nature to make the kind of cold military decision the Soviets made in Hungary. Despite the street fighting and the ferment, however, it is probably not going to hell. There is still goodness and greatness in this country and probably more compassion than is good for it tactically.

I don't like long-haired beatniks in the streets any more than you, but the protests are not all bad. The rosters in Vietnam are filled with unlucky ones who, in one way or another, were victimized by a bland middle-class notion about how we should select the people to do our dirty work when there is a fight but no glory.

It was not a corrupt favoritism, rather a casual and inherited one. You may have noticed there are not many glamorous people serving in Vietnam; that is, bigtime athletes or others similarly favored. This is changing, and the card-burners, even the whining and self-pitying ones, are having something to do with it.

Confessions of a Thoughtful Lover

STOCKHOLM, Sweden — She had skeptical blue eyes and a free-flowing figure that was slowed only occasionally by the legal requirements of clothing.

"The trouble with most American research people who want to know about sex-in-Sweden," she said, "is that they start out like professional scholars who turn out to be amateurish lovers."

"No doubt," her interrogator agreed. "In turn, you have one misconception here that ought to be corrected. Most Americans do not necessarily believe the Swedes invented sex. They simply believe you talk about it better and with fewer blushes, which is why your opinions are highly valued in these matters."

The young lady seemed appeased and our clinical discussion proceeded in good temper. She was blonde and, lifting her face languidly to the sun, settled into that type of hazy-eyed, Nordic trance that leaves you convinced you have just discovered the next million-dollar movie star — until you observe that almost all of them look that way over here, and it is all pretty overwhelming.

Her name was Anne-Marie. She filled up most of the showy part of the cafe window through which we viewed the afternoon promenade in the Berzelii Park. Professionally she functioned as a government receptionist but socially today she had agreed to advise the innocent American about sex and the Swedish girl — a topic almost impossible to escape here, whatever one's initial impulses.

"Yes," she said, "I have a fiance, with whom I go to bed from time to time. Why not? I would not have it any other way."

Instinctively, from the vigor with which the young lady spoke, one gathered this view was strongly endorsed by the fiance.

"This does not mean," she continued, "that I am typical of the young Swedish woman or not typical of her. It simply means that is what I prefer.

"Yes, there are such things as trial marriages and experimentation. A couple planning to get married, and wishing to live together beforehand, may find it hard to get an apartment and may stay together with the parents.

"I'm not sure how you define morals in America and I certainly know they don't agree about definitions over here. If my fiance and I love each other and want to share ourselves before we marry, that is our business and there is nothing dirty about it.

"We traveled together for a time in America and some of our friends there were horrified, not by our wanting to but because of the appearances.

"And so what does the difference in standards come to? You people no doubt do the same things the engaged couple will do over here, only you will do it with motels, and the trouble with that is that it is less convenient and more expensive."

Most Swedes will talk candidly and with some ardor about the subject partly because they have been educated to. The country is one of the few in the world where sex education is compulsory in the schools. Its hazards and potentials are discussed with spirit and occasionally belligerence from the pulpit, in front of a microphone and in various other public forums.

The Swedes don't agree on a moral code any more than the Americans or the Samoans do, but they do agree as a matter of state policy that young people should be instructed on sex questions, that all children are entitled to the same care and therefore no discrimination is allowed against children born out of wedlock; and that the husband and wife are to be considered equal partners in marriage, not only legally but in the physical satisfaction of the marriage act.

This, in turn, has resulted in a more casual and permissive attitude here and in other parts of Scandinavia toward the commercial side of sex.

Movie billboards, for example, will show a nude couple romping in bed. Pornography is effortlessly displayed in some of the photo shop windows.

One, called the Sexy Shop on Drottinggatan, promotes an exhibit in the basement by displaying magazine covers showing undressed women in spectacular attitudes.

The magazines, declared the English-born pornographist who sells in the shop, have to be cleared in some fashion by the government and presumably can be as specific as they want to in photography up to the point of showing actual physical union.

He was also selling film clips for $18, showing a gyrating young woman apparently working off her aggressions with a variety of imaginative moves.

"Let the perverts buy the stuff if that is what they need," the receptionist observed. "It is better for them to do that than to go around maiming children or stealing panties."

The traveler finds it almost impossible to argue with this kind of continental logic. Nor is he offended by many sights in this islanded city of castles, arbors, and money-making shops and skyscrapers.

The least offensive, of course, are the beautiful women — and it is probable that Sweden not only leads the league here but is never going to have to worry about magic numbers or a close pennant race.

Typically, they wear mini-skirts with long white hose. They are chicly dressed, in harmony with the country's high prosperity, and they may be svelte secretaries, fashionable housewives or far-out beatniks, but almost all of them look as though they ought to be sponsored on prime time television.

You will not see much evidence of prostitution in Stockholm — partly, the waggish natives will say, because the tourists couldn't afford it and partly, the waggish tourists might say, because of all the amateur competition.

There are pickup places here just as there are in Minneapolis, only here the practice seems to have achieved a good deal more style and finesse. Here the couple might strike up a conversation at the Prinsen cafe over a plate of pickled eel instead of a martini and peanuts at Webster's.

As for the women, the Englishman in the photo shop professed to give the authoritative view.

"There is one very strange thing about Swedish women," he said. "For 10 months of the year or so, no women in the world have as much ardor.

"But in the summer months, you may as well rent a hermitage. All they want in July and August is the sun. They will spend hours looking up at the sun or lying in it, because they do not get much of it the rest of the year."

A Wandering Fan Learns the Score

SOMEWHERE IN EUROPE – The most faithful courier in international commerce, the Swiss telephone service, put me back in the ballpark with the adventurous Twins a few hours ago after all else had failed, including the Associated Press and the yodelers' grapevine.

The Swiss telephones did it for 18 cents, less than the price of Calvin's popcorn, and in an elapsed time of two minutes. I have known box seat holders at Metropolitan Stadium who have spent more time and money getting the result direct from the scoreboard.

To appreciate the scope of the performance, you must understand the situation. I had last heard from the Twins when Sam Mele was on the mound changing pitchers. At the time I left, this particular move by Mele was not as much a tactic as a condition of employment. I went winging across the Atlantic and barging through the European fog wondering, "Has Mele changed yet, and if not, has Griffith changed yet?"

Under either set of circumstances, it looked perilous for Mele.

The Swiss, of course, do not understand baseball and, unlike the fans in Baltimore, admit it. You mention "pitcher" here, and they come at you with foaming beakers of Pilsener and avalanches of zither chords.

But my passions cried for news of the Twins. I was impelled to pick up a telephone in Zermatt, desposit the equivalent of five cents and ask, "Sprechen Sie English, Fraulein?"

She answered, "Nein," and it seemed rather permanent.

I don't know why I expected something more, except that I have come to lodge so much confidence in the Swiss' efficiency I was prepared to hear the operator tell me the Twins were out of their minds to bring in Ronnie Kline again.

Instead, she wanted to know who were the Twins – which most travelers will admit is not an original question.

Then I asked for the number of the Associated Press in Geneva. She wanted to know who was the Associated Press.

In my heart of hearts I know now the operator was teasing me for this harmless 15 seconds, amused by my linguistic floundering and blushing at the split in my infinitives. She gave me the numbers of the AP offices in Geneva and Zurich, the correspondent's home phones and the photography bureaus.

Nobody at the AP was home at 5:30 p.m. This made me heartsick as an AP alumnus. Surely, I mused, the AP in Switzerland has some kind of counterpart of the South St. Paul livestock report or the five-day weather forecasts to keep the authors off the streets until after the rush hours.

Quickly, I leafed through a Zurich directory in the telephone booth and found a number for United Press International.

"Bonjour," announced a man who later gave his name as Ernest Weilenmann.

I came at Weilenmann sidearm immediately. "The AP," I said, "cannot deliver the score of the Twins game last night against the Yankees. My recollection of UPI staffers is that they were rarely overpaid but at least they knew the score."

Weilenmann left the phone and was back in 10 seconds. "Twins 4, Yankees 3," he said, whereupon he began reading the account of the ball game, describing it as an uphill victory. The account had three typographical errors, and a sparseness of style that suggested it probably was edited by a soccer-playing telegrapher from Portugal. But it was more than the AP had.

"Who did you say made that error for the Twins?" I asked the UPI man.

"Solo Versailles," he said, making Zoilo sound like a broken treaty.

The coin machine logged 70 centimes, less than 20 cents for a call across three mountain ranges and nine chocolate factories. I bid the operator good night. She responded cheerily and never let on. But I would have sworn she mumbled to her switchboard mate as we were hanging up: "Kline must have had his spitter working last night, nicht wahr?"

'Dig for the Butt, Ol' Man'

The stub of a discarded cigarette is smoldering at his feet, on the muddy floor of the black patrol wagon carrying 16 men from the city jail to the workhouse.

There is not much left, enough to pinch between the thumb and middle finger for four or five drags.

He is in his 50's, wearing shredded overalls, a faded black-and-red wool shirt, a billed wool cap. His nose has been broken and rebroken and his face is pasty up to the faint alcoholic tinge in his cheeks.

He regards the cigarette stub absently, reaches into the dirt of the wagon floor and picks it up. His eyes shift slightly to the side in a fugitive glance to see whether anyone is watching this small surrender of his remaining pride, and some are. But it does not matter and he drags on the cigarette, hungrily.

A wisecracking auto thief sitting next to me explodes into unmanageable laughter. "Lookit the ole man," he howls. "Look where he got the butt, off that lousy ole floor. Hey, ole man, whyn't you go on television and give one of those commercials about likin' it better."

His buddies, the swingers in the paddy wagon claque, join the laughter.

The broken-nosed drifter at the end of the bench does not change expression but he is uneasy under the hooting ridicule, scraping his boots slowly on the floor in an aimless, futile misery. He cups the dregs of the cigarette in his hand but we all know it is still there and so is his shame. But there is one more drag left in the cigarette, so he will not drop the butt until he has had it.

There are a couple of workhouse regulars who know him on today's paddy wagon run and they don't smile; but they do wish the man would stiffen his back and call his taunters the names that fit.

He finishes his cigarette and the wagon skids out of an intersection on Highway 55, wheels past the Golden Valley shopping center, past the Beacon Heights Elementary School of Plymouth, the attractive suburban residential tract, and toward the stone-and-brick institution on Parker's Lake.

The wise guy next to me has half-finished his long Viceroy cigarette and, after drawing our attention, flips it at the feet of the bum at the end of the wagon. He sees it but does not move. The auto thief is smiling brilliantly and imperiously, but the shabby drifter still has a grain of dignity left.

He will not perform for the thief or the rest of the baiting audience. So the thief moves over and nudges the stub closer.

I have had about enough of this grandstanding sadism and reach for the thief's arm. The old drifter turns now, however, and looses a flood of profanity on his tormentor. It is not very cohesive and it is not even very good profanity but they all laugh. One of the young hood's pals takes a fresh pack of cigarettes from his pocket and, cordially, offers the bum a whole one.

The bum accepts with a silent nod. I have the impression he is actually thanking the unknown benefactor for restoring his pride. But I conclude finally that all he is doing is thanking him for a few fresh drags.

Most of the passengers today have spent time in the workhouse before, not only the drunken repeaters but a couple of parole violators, petty-coin thieves and the wild drivers.

The aspiring hood next to me had led the catcall section when the patrol wagon drove past bannering police near the courthouse.

"What in the hell those lazy clowns done to deserve more money?" he says. "The only trouble with cops in most big towns is they're on the wrong side of the bars. This town, they're not only clowns but stupid. They get chances to make money but they're too Boy Scout to take it. So they rather walk around the block with signs like the world is mean to them instead of taking dough when it's there for the askin'.

"You know what else gives me a belly laugh? The judge sittin' there tellin' you all about the misery that alcohol causes in the world and how even if it doesn't wreck you it will fuzz your thinkin'. And then them sittin' around havin' lunch with the big shots and drinkin' their two or three martinis before goin' back to the courthouse.

"If I was the cops I'd have a drink or two with my own lunch. Why the hell not? The judges do it. So do the big shot executives and all the white-collar clowns and even the ministers if nobody is watchin' them.

"So who the hell makes up the rules, anyway?"

The drunks in the van have been here too often to pretend excuses.

The younger ones here, however, have stronger passions, deeper resentments, a noisier cynicism, an angrier sense of persecution and, in the case of the man in jail for the first time, a deeper hurt and ignominy.

They gossip about the judges, "the good guy" judges and "the bastard judges."

They wear the garments in which they were arrested and in which they slept overnight in the tank. There is a junkyard worker with grime and grease in his stinking clothes and larceny never far from his mind.

"When they picked me up Saturday night," he is telling a denim-clad workhouse regular, "I was just a coupla hours away from a $6,000 box job."

"The cops did you a favor," the workhouser says.

"The cops did themselves a favor," the other says, "because I coulda opened the door with my hands and it's a pushover."

The workhouse inmate views the nondescript colony around him with the pro's tolerance of the novice plugger.

"Some guy asks me how it's been in the workhouse," he says. "You can have it. Me, I'm lonesome. All my old buddies are up at Stillwater, where I'm headin' myself. There are a coupla guys at the workhouse I knew in St. Cloud (reformatory) but they don't mean nuthin' to me."

My heart manages a faint but brief flutter for this abandoned soul, one of the more accomplished forgers and check artists in the community. I am more interested, however, in the gabby, curly-haired Minneapolis kid who has been sweating down the bench.

He had spent the better part of Saturday night in the courthouse tank narrating an account of his walk-away from the workhouse.

"I'm workin' on this see-ment detail and I just go over the wall. My girl is waitin' for me in the car there on the road by the workhouse, and man, I'm hungry if you know what I mean, and I'm still hungry when we get to her place. I figure it's all worth it even though they pick me up on 10th and Hennepin couple nights later. Now I ain't so sure."

But he had come bounding back into the chute after his

appearance on the escape charge, and now he was ecstatic to the point of incoherence, his mouth a blur, chewing his gum and frothing his good fortune.

"What do you think of that byootiful judge," he says. "Ten days is all I get. Man, I mean I put the words on that judge. I'm shakin' all the time but I got the whole thing laid out for him, like how I got all this hard time in the workhouse and the other guys are trying to get me, and I been applying for everything, the Huber Law, probation, parole, bad health. I mean I got to get out of there for pure survival, your honor, and so I got no choice but to run.

"You know what I was lookin' at. I was lookin' at 90 days more but the judge says ten, and brother I could kiss that black robe of his.

"I felt like laughin' out loud because I'm so lucky and happy. And I thought all judges were bastards. Well, they are, but this was a good one."

He says confidentially, "I don't mind admittin' that I was praying hard, man. I mean really praying."

I ask whether he is going to offer a prayer of thanksgiving now.

"I don't know any of those," he says. "All I know is I got only 247 days left now."

The workhouse vet smiles at the amateurish performance.

"You wanna know something really chicken?" he says. "I'm doin' all this time in the workhouse, a year, and they're gonna hit me with another charge when I finish, so that I'm goin' to Stillwater, and they brought me down here from the workhouse because I don't pay a traffic ticket.

"Imagine? A traffic ticket. And you know what they give me for it? Five days. Five days, and me with all that time. I hope the clowns are very happy, and I hope they remember those things when the rich fatheads get off from doin' time because they got a lawyer and everybody drinks martinis together at the club and the slobs like us get time."

"Some guys," he admits, "are born losers. I had a buddy who needed bail money real bad. He sends his best pal after his bail money, which he keeps in his room, and the buddy not only makes off with the bail money but the guy's girl."

"Boys," he says philosophically, "a man has just one helluva time stayin' even with the game."

Two men in uniform come and herd the shabby van colony. In front of the workhouse vet is a young man just sentenced to a year for narcotics possession. The workhouse vet apes his captors behind their backs. But the young man is handcuffed to another inmate, and he is weeping aloud.

Carry Your Shovels Proudly, People

You may have heard that robins have been sighted in Hopkins, parts of Wayzata and as far north as Brooklyn Center.

Granted, they did not tarry and are now feathering northward toward International Falls, where the winter has been milder.

But watchers insisted their tracks are unmistakable, prompting the breathless question: "With robins on the wing, can those other faithful messengers of spring – rotting ice and yawning chuck holes – be far behind?"

I think not, and in view of this I think it is time for a summing-up, a serious self-examination, to find out what psychological changes have been wrought in our people by the scourge of this most unforgettable winter.

I'm not suggesting it's over just because there's a little pool of dirty brown melt-water out in the parking lot. But it is the small things like these on which hope and the onward sweep of the human spirit are built.

We will get more blizzards routinely and we will get our record snowfall and we will get exasperated anew, but I'm sure future historians will record that nothing ennobled and tempered the Twin Cities dweller as the winter of 1966-67.

It has imparted, for example, an entire new dimension to our culture. The once-humble snow shovel has achieved a status beyond the wildest vision of its designer.

The disclosure that snow shoveling, done in moderation, can stimulate a person erotically has produced a revolution almost overnight in at least one of our social symbols. As a trademark of man's bedroom prowess, the hairy chest has now been replaced by the upraised spade.

True, the implications are staggering. One strong blizzard, for instance, may some day undo an entire year's hard work by the Planned Parenthood Society.

The winter has worked a congealing effect on the drive for unity between Minneapolis and St. Paul, once merely a dream but now a real and alarming possibility. We have discovered we are actually brothers under the same insulated underwear, that we all pull on our anti-slush boots one at a time.

In short, I'd say we have been graced and uplifted by the Four Canons of a Cataclysmic Climate – candor, calm, compassion and co-operation. To illustrate, in order:

Candor – Housewives now quite frankly are confronting their husbands at the doorway with shovel in hand and a challenging look. On the other hand, a Minneapolis woman writes to the editor declaring she is shoveling so much snow as to risk the label of nymphomaniac but all she has to show for it so far is a sore back. The point is, our people are now baring their souls, and never mind the condition of their backs.

Calm – "I admit I am disturbed by a new game being played by motorists around here, snowbank roulette," writes the insurance companies' watchdog, Robert Provost. "But I really didn't appreciate the other side of the Twin Cities' winter character, coolness under pressure, until I visited Chicago. They tell me motorists deserted their cars by the thousands in their big storm, left them in the streets, on the highways, in the middle of intersections. Here, all they do is stay with their cars and swear."

Compassion – Our people DO care, not only about other people but about the sensibilities of the uncomplaining machines. "Yes, the weather clocks may give us conflicting readings in downtown Minneapolis," writes Bob Evans, "but they have been rather faithful sentinels for all that, and with nothing to look forward to but an annual oil change and a new coat of paint, can we wonder at their simple expressions of personality toward the weather?" Evans is right, of course. Go ahead, weather clocks, have your independence.

Co-operation – I used to think there was nothing wrong with St. Paul that couldn't be cured by a time machine. Attitudes change. The winter has covered our old enmities. St. Paul has made the streets safe for Swedes and needs only to do the same now for Republicans. We now use the same underground shelters against the storm, the same translator for Calvin Griffith. Some day we will get together on that capstone of our new civic harmony, the big league zoo.

I think we should be very, very proud.

The Sweat-Sock Elite and Vietnam

Unexpectedly, I discovered a new side to TV's versatile genius this weekend — that it can protect the traveler against attacks of the psychological bends when he surfaces into his old environment.

For the man who is emotionally unready to return to the asphalt society after 10 days of rodeos, make-believe corral gunfights and other prairie circuses, TV this weekend offered a suitable transition: A hairy, cliff-hanging spectacle in which two grown men in Twins' uniforms try to ambush an infield fly at breakneck speeds from opposite directions in the ninth inning.

The net result was to give first baseman Rich Reese the distinction of making a violent campaign out of an easy popup. Confronted with heroics on this scale, one tends to forget quickly the relatively tame achievements of the Brahma bull riders.

Turning to another channel, the viewer discovers we have in our midst a golf course called Hazeltine near Chaska, so fierce and vast as to be shunned by the best golfers in the world and to be unnavigable to the others. One of the high-ranked contestants came off the final green waving the ball in imperial triumph, giving him the appearance of some kind of niblicked Attila. I learned later that he was celebrating finishing two over par. The weary and desperate manner of the other finishers raised the serious question of whether they were playing the Minnesota Classic at Hazeltine or at Wold-Chamberlain airport.

All of this reassures me that big-time sports, for all the grimness and large money that has been grafted onto it by its promoters, is still the fantasyland of American culture. I say this reassures me, because some of the athletic prodigies and much of the public tend to forget it.

This would be harmless if it did not bump into the more serious business of military obligations and how they are fulfilled at a time when the country is involved in an interminable armed struggle in which hundreds of anonymous kids, some of them highly unathletic, are getting their heads shot off.

They were not necessarily any more patriotic than the luckier young men who are serving their military time in National

Guard camps or in reserve units. But I do wonder about the propriety of major league ballplayers commuting between camp and the ballfield while the nameless kids— whose employers did not have the influence or the urgency to get them tucked away safely — are filling up the rosters for Vietnam.

There is no moral judgment here. The draftees in Vietnam would eagerly take the same arrangement if handed to them. But we should have no illusions about the string-pulling of the past, some of it condoned by the military and much of it ignored by the public.

This has happened partly because of the peculiarly romanticized status conferred on the big-time athlete in a country where he has been lionized, idolized, subsidized and publicly simonized. There are, of course, as many saints and sinners in his business as there are in yours or mine. There are extremely noble and responsible people in the nation's clubhouses, and there are also overgrown thumbsuckers who have already been measured for the baggy-pants version of Valhalla.

All that is being asked here is that they should be required to line up and take their chances with the rest. That they have not for the last few years is partly the responsibility of the newspapers, which for decades did not report sports so much as they propagandized it, pandered for it and apologized for it.

Some time ago the newspapers began paying their employes a living wage and spared them the necessity of taking money from the organizations about which they reported. This emancipation has now reached almost all major newspapers.

Their ticket-selling function, accordingly, has been taken over by and large by the radio and television stations which broadcast the ball games.

And so there is still a dream-world quality to the broad arena of American sports, although a certain amount of realism is starting to intrude.

I find this encouraging. This plus the fact that the most popular athletic hero of the weekend turned out to be a middle-aged golfer named Julius Boros — who did not win but who proved you can make $100,000 looking like a prosperous butcher strolling down the fairway.

Lutherans at Loggerheads

Lovers of intramural warfare can only admire the ingenuity and fierceness with which the battle was waged this weekend for control of the huge Lutheran Brotherhood insurance society.

It used to be that when Lutherans quarreled the result was a new synod or another picnic at Mount Olivet Lutheran Church.

But the stakes were enormously higher Friday, and the emotions deeper, demanding the last reserves of generalship, stamina and cunning on both sides. And it is with some mingled fondness and regret, therefore, that I must report on the pivotal tactic of the long day's struggle:

Somebody locked the door to the Lutheran Brotherhood Building's gold-plated men's room, the one sanctuary of neutrality where the warring slates of directors could meet on common ground in a spirit of good will and forbearance.

The report is verified by spokesmen for both sides in addition to a neutral janitor who had passed through that portion of the building in a relatively high state of urgency. Its authenticity, accordingly, is beyond dispute.

It's useless to speculate on what set of circumstances, or what degree of bitterness, would drive a man to lock out of the men's room not only his fraternal enemies but his colleagues as well.

The only unchallengeable conclusion is that when the Lutherans fight among themselves, they play rough.

Fraternal strife among the Catholics is romper room stuff in comparison. When Catholics have battled, it has been over such trivia as papal abuse of indulgences, the keys to the kingdom, control of medieval armies, should priests marry, the Notre Dame schedule or the Milton Berlesque sermons of Father Fleming at St. Olaf's.

When Jews battled each other, on the other hand, there has always been much uncertainty because they have never stayed in the same place long enough to determine who has the home field advantage. The upshot, therefore, usually has been another clothing store on Hennepin Avenue.

And so let us briefly reconstruct the angry events leading up to that unorthodox maneuver yesterday. You must be aware that the longtime chief executive, Carl F. Granrud, was rebuffed in his bid for re-election last month. He accused his enemies on the board of "scheming, plotting and conniving."

To which opponent A. Herbert Nelson replied, in the same spirit of Christian moderation that had characterized Granrud's remarks: "(Lutherans) want eradicated forever the tyranny, dictatorship, rule by fear and favor, the wasting of Lutheran Brotherhood earnings on self-glorification, such as went on for the last several years."

Now these are not bad for openers in any Christian dialogue. At the same time they do represent, as one awed bystander observed, a helluva way to get to heaven.

In any event, another facedown meeting between the two forces was scheduled yesterday in the beautiful and lofty Brotherhood Building. This is the green-marbled and excitingly-paned downtown tower which also houses offices of the city's dynamic Chamber of Commerce leaders and therefore is described in some quarters as "The Glass Menagerie."

By court order, Granrud was barred from the building. What the Nelson forces had overlooked, apparently, was that the ousted chief executive was carrying with him not only a good deal of resentment, but also the only readily-accessible key to the gold-trimmed men's room that had been the board's pride for some time.

"Either he's got it," one of Granrud's opponents muttered acidly, "or one of his sympathizers has got it. It's hard to imagine a man being that vengeful."

And yet, without our taking sides in the issue, can the neutralists truly blame the Granrud forces for this resourceful ploy? I mean they DID lock the man out of his own building.

But I know there is enough humanity in our hearts to sympathize with both parties in this predicament. Philosophically, we can note that in almost every struggle conducted on this scale of ferocity and vindictiveness, it is the innocent who must suffer.

Militarily, I do not know how this maneuver would be classified. Strategically, I suppose, it would come under the broad general heading of a holding action. Ultimately, the Granrud forces lost.

But the battle, if long, at least was suspenseful.

A Letter to Iceland

His Excellency, the ambassador to Iceland, has appealed to his former constituents in Minnesota to drop him a line and to keep him informed of what is going on in his old romping room, the State Capitol.

I'm sure Mr. Rolvaag realizes that this service, if performed, would put the former governor at least two jumps ahead of his former constituents.

It's true, however, that Mr. Rolvaag's post in Reykjavik, south of the volcanoes, is somewhat outside the normal trade routes. When we read that the ex-governor has learned little of what has been happening in Minnesota, we have to sympathize with his twinge of homesickness. It wasn't so long ago, after all, when Minnesota was receiving twice-weekly mail deliveries. There are places such as Minneapolis where we still do not have regular snowplow service.

And so, in a spirit of kinship I have written to Mr. Rolvaag seeking to explain, as best as I have been able to decode it, what has been happening in the Capitol:

"Mr. Rolvaag. I trust you have fitted smoothly into the confusion of lefthand driving in Iceland, in view of your training in the Minnesota Statehouse and the DFL party.

"You may have discovered some time after the last election that Minnesota has a $100 million surplus.

"Accordingly, the lawmakers are going to move into June with their special session in an aggressive effort bent on figuring out new ways to tax us.

"Otherwise, the situation is about as you and Mr. Keith left it. Naturally, there have been a few major achievements. The legislature already has established a record for revolving door legislation by passing the sales tax four times and at this very writing is going for five.

"Since the last courier passed through Reykjavik, however, you should know it has now been decided to exempt coffins from the sales tax. Most of the voters, Mr. Rolvaag, regard this as a commendable step forward, although it does tend to confirm the theory that you have got to be dead before you get a tax break nowadays.

"I think the bedrock intent behind this particular exemption, however, is to spare us the odd fractions in grave-digging. Whoever heard of having to go 3 per cent past 6 feet?

"At the same time, the bill-writers decided not to exempt certain religious symbols from the tax, presumably reasoning that God is probably a Republican, or at least a Conservative, and will understand.

"Your successor, Harold LeVander, has doggedly kept his pledge not to sign a sales tax that does not require a vote by the taxpayers. The Republican professionals maintain nobody should be that pure politically. The Democrats, of course, have maintained it all along. The Republicans, therefore, are voting against the Republican governor, and the Democrats are voting with him.

"Karl, I just know you would have been in your element in these circumstances. I think you will be encouraged to learn that Mr. LeVander has done very well in his training program in verbal acrobatics.

"Mr. LeVander signed the Sunday liquor bill on the grounds that the people have a right to decide locally whether they want to buy booze with their Sunday chicken.

"He signed the Sunday closing bill on the grounds that the people ought to stay together on Sundays and should not be lured into iniquitous discount stores where they would be tempted to buy such unsabbatical commodities as binoculars, ping pong sets, and harmonicas.

"This will free them to patronize, among other places, restaurants selling booze. The trouble here is that downtown Minneapolis has been supporting the Sunday liquor option — and as a civilized sort of thing, I favor it myself — partly to keep some of the business now being siphoned off by Wisconsin.

"Mr. Rolvaag, it would be cruel and inhuman if Minneapolis voted down Sunday liquor and the Minneapolis business went to Michael's in Rochester, Nybo's in Red Wing and the sausage foundries in New Ulm, instead of Somerset and Hudson in Wisconsin.

"Otherwise, things here are normal. We are bringing in more gadfly geniuses to tell us all about our hodge-podge environment and will do our level best to spend our money in a manner of which the architects may be proud."

The Pilot Is Dropped

Calvin Griffith is the only man I know who could rout the Israelis, Nasser, and the United Nations from the top of the front page in the middle of an international crisis.

Admittedly, the Twins' ratings in the press and on television and radio had been losing ground steadily to the U.N. the past week, at a time when the Twins' attendance ought to be soaring. Killebrew hit five home runs in four days, but the fans were talking about Moshe Dayan.

Accordingly, Griffith was driven to the panic point when Nasser's field-reversing gymnastics threatened to overshadow the Twins in the same way the Vikings managed it two years ago.

Then, you will recall, the coach quit after the team was demolished by Baltimore. Griffith is slyly perceptive in these things and could see the parallel developing in Cairo. The Arabs are overrun by the Israelis. Nasser quits, contending he could take the Arabs so far but couldn't get them over the sand dunes and into the Super Oasis.

Two years ago the Viking board of directors came to the coach and talked him out of quitting, extending him a five-year contract as balm.

It was clear to Griffith the Egyptian National Assembly was going to do the same thing for Nasser, thus permitting him to go into training for another rematch two years from now, when he will again be demolished by the Israelis.

Griffith was not going to let Nasser get away with it and forthwith fired Sam Mele as manager, replacing him with a man named Cal Ermer, who promptly disclosed to us Friday night that "the name of the game is win."

I would regard this as a routinely sophomoric observation from a rookie big league manager except that Mr. Ermer ought to be corrected at a very early stage and be reminded the name of the game is to make money. Calvin senses the fans' enthusiasm for the Twins has paled in recent months, a situation which can tend to lower profits and is, therefore, painful to Mr. Griffith.

The fans clearly needed some new and giddy stimulation and Calvin unerringly has provided it by hiring Cal Ermer. One of the objectives here undoubtedly is to invest the ball games with a fresh, free-wheeling excitement. The Twins made a hopeful start in this direction by giving the fans a 13-run ballgame in Ermer's debut.

Unfortunately, 11 of these runs belonged to Baltimore. The new manager did, however, provide encouraging evidence of avoiding one of Mele's reputed sins, which was to ride too long with a struggling pitcher. Ermer removed Jim Perry promptly with the bases congested in the fifth inning. His successor, Jim Ollom, immediately entered into the gala spirit of the high-scoring evening by serving a three-run home run to Frank Robinson.

None of this, I'm sure you understand, is intended to underview Ermer's abilities as a manager, which no doubt are considerable. He is to be wished success, by friends and critics of Mele alike.

But the listener and viewer does tend to retch mildly when hearing the house-announcer version of events on radio and TV. Mele, you may recall, was largely ignored at a time when he was in bad odor with Griffith and when this was understood by the people who are describing the games.

Griffith now has a new boy as manager and is anxious for a happy reception for him. Thus we heard the new manager's strategy described as "terrific" last night when he walked Frank Robinson to bring up Boog Powell. The strategy may have been good or it may have been sound, in the same way that it is good and sound to use any device short of an ICBM to keep Robinson away from the plate.

It was a few degrees less than terrific, however, inasmuch as Powell planted the ball into the right field seats for three runs.

Calvin Griffith is not a bad nor sinister person, and while his thrift is fun to josh, he is not an irredeemable nickel-squeezer. Nobody close to baseball really quarrels with his logic in removing Sam at a point when Mele did not have firm control of the club.

Sam Mele was a capable, winning manager but beyond this an immensely decent man. The wonder is that he survived so long in view of the casual knifing and intramural club gossip directed at him by people within the official and touring family, including those supposed friends of Mele.

A Calm Day on the Mountain

The presence of a minister in a climbing party is one of those small luxuries of mountaineering. It may not be an open-end guarantee of safety, but at least it is a comforting hedge.

"I could kick myself," the Rev. Tom Smatla confided, "for not bringing along a copy of the Sermon on the Mount. I always like to read it before going on a climb."

I nodded, sharing his regret. "No doubt such a passage from the good book would be very suitable," I agreed. "Right now, however, I would settle for 120 feet of rope. Ultimately I would like to inherit the earth. My only ambition at present is to hang onto it."

The reverend smiled vaguely and looked skyward with benevolence. It was hard to determine whether he was admiring the 12,500-foot mass of Mt. Moran or seeking a ray of tolerance from the high command.

He was good and diverting company on the half hour walk through the leafy, shade-darkened Teton underbrush en route to Leigh Lake. The reverend preferred rambling monologues about the origin of the dusty white mushrooms underfoot, delivered either by himself or the other two, professional guide Herb Swedlund or Monte Later, a shopkeeper-naturalist from St. Anthony, Idaho.

Silently, I regarded much of this fungus philosophy as clearly unbalanced.

For an hour we rowed the deep jade of Leigh Lake beneath the bulking immensity of Moran, a mountain outreached by two or three peaks in the Grand Tetons but easily the most massive and complicated in the range in breadth, in the gendarmed architecture of its system of pinnacled satellites and in pure geology.

The noon sun lay open the sandy lake floor 25 feet below the little skiff. There would be no clouds today, and not much relief on the high-angled approach-drag to an overnight camp in the Douglas firs 4,000 feet above.

We covered it in a leisurely four hours, up acres of tall sunflowers, fields of slag dumped down the slopes of Moran through the eons of the mountain's housekeeping chores and finally into the sweet pine fragrance of the camp.

A couple of miles away the broad, tabled summit of Moran

hung in the sky. The predictable schooners of clouds were cruising eastward above the Tetons and into the canyons by now, but the weather held idyllic.

The Tetons are not conventional mountains. There are no definable foothills here to play a toadying counterpoint to the imperial sweep of the higher summits. The mountains explode out of the valley, lofting more than a mile above the floor at their highest reach.

Whatever his experience in mountain country, they touch the viewer with clashing senses of excitement and anxiety. Even in innocent sunlight there is a kind of desperate beauty in the spiked virility of these mountains. They ARE beautiful, and the seasoned Teton climber will stand among them affectionately. But in the rain or hail or descending darkness, they may also scare the hell out of him.

Swedlund, neatly bearded and youthful despite eight years of guiding in the range, lit his primus cooker and we had supper of soup, fruit, and sandwiches. The sun eased over the western rim of the range at 8:30. We made tea over a campfire and Monte Later, a big and powerful westerner who brought to the mountains a twangy scholarship, talked for a half hour on geology and origin of the Tetons.

The reverend Tom now presided for a few minutes on the natural wonders of Bemidji, Minn., where he served a Presbyterian congregation for 15 years before moving to Butte, Mont. He was 52 years old, somewhat out of condition, but a competent and wide-eyed climber who was inclined to give the rope an evangelical chewing-out when it got hung up over a crag.

We rolled into our sleeping bags, two of us under the fir boughs and the other two under a makeshift plastic canopy. The air was warm and calm. The lights died in the valley miles away and the only sound was a vagrant puff of wind against the plastic shelter. The smell of the pine was pure perfume.

I nudged the reverend at 4 a.m. "It's time," I observed, "to rouse the other parishioners." No light was necessary two hours before sunrise. The enormous moon floated over us, a fat white pumpkin blowing out the stars.

We resumed the scree and meadow trudge above the camp, rounded Moran's west horn, a needled appendage to the mountain, and in two hours reached the gateway to the climb itself, another outcrop known to the mountaineers as Drizzlepuss.

Swedlund uncoiled the ropes here and we linked up. Drizzlepuss opened the door to the climb, but we had to descend 200 feet as part of the maneuver. Except for a damp sleeping bag, nothing is more maddening on a mountain than having to lose altitude in mid-climb.

We had come up a mile vertically from the valley and now we viewed head-on the mountain's last dimensions – hundreds of feet of high-pitched slabs on Moran's east face where, from this aspect, there appeared to be few stable footholds or handholds.

"Also," Swedlund informed us amiably, "the snowbridge between Drizzlepuss and the East Face is gone and we are going to have to grope around to find our way onto it."

This accomplished, we mounted the slabs.

The holds were there, everywhere. The rock was firm and the friction underfoot, even at pitches of 50 degrees and more, welded you to the mountain.

Moran's vastness kept deceiving us. On our right was a long, distinctive outcropping of basalt, a dike that bisected the mountain from its summit to the Falling Ice glacier in the cirque below. The summit was coming down to us, all right, but it took three hours to reach us.

The reverend erupted occasionally in his crusade against the rope's impish heresy. "Tom," Later yelled, "why in hell get mad at the rope? Save it for collection time."

The reverend paused, apparently in another providential appeal, after which I would have sworn I heard him tell Later where he would like to see him go if the big westerner had no preference.

The sweat, however, flowed faster than the dialogue. At 11:30 we kicked into a snow cornice, climbed up its 10 foot overhang and walked onto the flat-topped summit of Moran, a bouldered wilderness of broken sedimentary rock stretching for nearly a half mile.

We shook hands, agreeably viewed the green mosaic of forest, lakes and sage of the valley, and idled for an hour in simple repose. There were no theatrics today, no fears, no sliding snow.

It was just a day on a mountain. It did not have to be anything else.

War in the Swamps

I hope you have not ignored the significance of the parallel announcements made this week by Gen. William C. Westmoreland and A. W. Buzicky, who commands the Metropolitan Mosquito Control District.

Neither — in the fashion of all generals — has enough men. Buzicky trails Westmoreland in jet bombers but leads in power sprayers and gets no worse than a draw in helicopters.

Moreover, they are virtually even in the politics of public relations. Westmoreland managed to recruit another 100,000 troops by outflanking Defense Secretary Robert McNamara, and Buzicky very subtly has convinced us of the need for more funds with his militant communiques of the last 10 days.

Undoubtedly you read figures Friday from the mosquito district showing only $264 is allotted a square mile in the battle against Twin Cities mosquitoes, compared with $2,000 for some cities elsewhere. Buzicky quite brazenly is appealing to nationalism and civic pride here and — in intimate conversation with me yesterday — added a new technique, the scare story.

"I am not being melodramatic about this," he confided. "The aedes vexan mosquito with which we are contending is one of the toughest, longest-flying, most aggressive and tautly disciplined mosquitoes in insect weaponry.

"The question is, can we really afford halfway measures in dealing with it?"

I am an innocent in this and cannot tell you whether we are involved with some kind of super-mosquito capable of visiting unprecedented damage and disability upon our people. I only know that even the most thick-skinned among us have to protest the lengths to which the mosquito people have gone to take advantage of our gullibility.

In other words, they have been at this mosquito control business on an areawide, saturation basis for 10 years. They have employed thousands of dollars worth of equipment and yet for all of the press releases about frontal attacks and new offensives, you are left with only one possible reading of the 10-year-old struggle:

The mosquitoes are still ahead!

"It's the potholes," said Buzicky.

"I beg your pardon," I interrupted.

"The potholes. They are worse in this region than they are in a place like Chicago or Toledo, where an outlay of $2,000 a square mile is common.

"You claim we are still losing," he continued, "but let me tell you, it was much worse at times three and four years ago, when the situation was so urgent we were literally concealing things from the public for fear of setting off mass alarm and demoralization. There was one year there where they very nearly overwhelmed us, when faint-hearts were heard in the counties calling for a return to smudge pots, 6-20 and cookout bans. It would have made places like Edina unlivable. These were the years of true and rare dedication among our men."

I often have wondered how wives of the mosquito control crews sent their men into the swamps. Whether, with a brave little smile, they would snap down the face nets of their warrior husbands, affectionately chuck them under the chins and in parting say with soft dignity, "Don't let them shaft you in the sloughs today."

"For weeks," Buzicky continued, "it was touch and go this year. For a while the only counter-action we could take was to adulticize them."

"It sounds," I said, "like an unnatural act."

"On the contrary, it was a campaign aimed at getting the older, veteran mosquitoes and was economical, in addition. The problem was how to save the most skin for a finn."

By such endearing drolleries does the mosquito district seek to humanize itself to the public. For several years, I understand, the secretary answered the phone not, "Hello," but, "Bzzzz, this is the mosquito control district."

"In any event," Buzicky said, "our sampling light traps have now disclosed a count falling from the 750 a couple of days ago to 150 yesterday. We can now fairly say we are over the hump, although we may not be out of the woods."

I'm not quite sure I can keep up with those quick shifts in terrain and it may be we need a surveyor more than a sprayer. The home-fronters behind the lines, general, are still loyal but in a frame of mind described by most psychologists as damned itchy.

Hubert at the Mike

Hubert Humphrey's sudden emergence as a sports announcer may have surprised radio listeners but did not surprise his Washington cronies, who have always classified Hubert as the Joe Garagiola of politics.

People in the trade inform me that Humphrey – with characteristic verve – already has achieved a first in the industry by becoming the only baseball broadcaster who not only forgot to pause for station identification but absolutely refused.

Under these conditions you would normally expect the Republicans to ask for equal time. It has not worked out that way. The first to ask for equal time was Herb Carneal, who is supposed to be broadcasting the games. Carneal made the appeal because Humphrey has placed him in what amounts to double jeopardy, inasmuch as Carneal already spends half his time trying to fend off Halsey Hall.

Accidentally I tuned in on the Twins over my transistor radio in Stockholm the other day while fumbling with the dial for the latest herring boat arrivals. It was the vice-president over the Voice of America, where he normally serves as Lyndon Johnson's color announcer. I did not object to Hubert's aimless blabbering for two innings, this being more or less occupational fare in the trade. I would, however, have appreciated a little more precise information, such as the score of the game.

Because of my past affection for him, I have a hard time putting down Humphrey as simply another limelight-grabbing politician, although I realize this is how he is behaving at the moment.

In this situation, you have to exercise some understanding. For the last three years Humphrey has had to struggle for his share of the national audience and has settled for subsidiary notices in the Washington press. He is, however, warmly known for his adaptability and therefore has acquired his primary prominence as a White House frug dancer who charms the bracelets off visiting dowagers from Liechtenstein.

He also logs some time dispensing tranquilizers to the President, and occasionally opens Nancy Dickerson's fan mail. The vice-president also makes speeches, although this is not so much a function as an instinct.

Otherwise, the vice-presidency appears to be a blight on this good man's energies, and we find him lately conducting a kind of unsponsored Johnny Carson show in the middle of the Twins-Cleveland series.

You should understand it has been a long and trying road to the broadcasting booth for Humphrey, requiring an extended apprenticeship in such menial positions as college professor, mayor of Minneapolis, U. S. senator and the vice-presidency. But he has finally arrived at the summit of the orator's calling, which means as a sports announcer he can now tell us why Ermer manages to keep Zimmerman on the bench at moments when the rest of his catching staff is chasing Worthington's sliders to the backstop.

Professionally, I would put Humphrey somewhere between Bill Stern and John Blanchard, meaning he has Stern's gift of imagination and John's flair for repetition.

He does not have the velocity of Dick Enroth nor Hall's volcanic spontaneity, but there is nothing wrong with his volume. Nor with his change of pace. Humphrey has that rare talent of being able to shift, in mid-syllable, from aid for France to aid for Chance.

Personally, however, I have to believe he would be a good deal more valuable to the Twins chasing Worthington's slider.

Nobody is going to contend the vice-president shouldn't enjoy a ball game as much as the rest of us. The difference, however, is that most of the customers are content to let Killebrew autograph the baseballs, Carneal do the broadcasting and Eddie Stanky do the grandstanding.

Aside from this, there is congestion enough listening to the ball game. Thus we have a roster that already includes Carneal, Hall, Harmon, Jagoe, Merriman, Hartman, Ermer, and occasionally the visiting relatives, to say nothing of the Hamm's brewing company, which is no longer appealing to our taste buds but simply appeals now to our gluttony.

In these circumstances, Mr. Humphrey, I'm sure you will agree we do not need a pause as much as an anesthetic. The alternative is to make a deal with the Twins whereby you do the broadcasting and Calvin makes the keynote address at the 1968 Democratic convention.

The nation, Mr. Humphrey, indeed lives in perilous times.

Strife in High Society

We are awash today with some of the most brilliant names in international politics and party-chasing, prompting intimate observers to raise the serious question:

Can the tigresses of Twin Cities' society get through the evening without civil war, hair-pulling or similar acts of impulsive violence that characterize red-blooded Minnesota girls who put on four competing parties?

You must be aware by now that at various functions tonight we are being graced by the appearance of Mrs. Lyndon Johnson, Mrs. Hubert Humphrey, the Orville Freemans and the British ambassador; by a banquet honoring the new president of the University of Minnesota; and by the return of the well-known resin bag party-goers, Bob Allison and Billy Martin.

Only the most reckless will attempt to arrange all of these luminaries into any kind of workable priority. And yet for all of the surface festivity and warm geniality, it must be reported for the record that rarely in the history of Twin Cities' society have the rival guest lists been compiled in an atmosphere of such relentless infighting and militant secrecy.

Loyalties are being examined and tested down to the very marrow. Agonized decisions have confronted some of the most important social figures in town. Imagine the dilemma of Miss Barbara Flanagan, for example, required to make a spontaneous decision if she were standing in the middle of the room and four doors opened, admitting Cary Grant, the Duke of Windsor, Nelson Rockefeller, and John Cowles.

The riddle: To whom would Miss Flanagan turn first?

We can only speculate. All we can ascertain definitely here in the plant is Miss Flanagan was so overwhelmed by this largesse of celebrities that she used up all of the bold-face type yesterday, creating a typographical crisis in the composing room.

While none will admit it publicly, the collision of parties, testimonials and banquets has produced a condition of chaos and intramural strife that has aroused conjecture suggesting the whole thing is sponsored and chaired by Mrs. Walter Butler.

I have heard serious suspicions of trading among the guest lists, wherein the Friends of the Minneapolis Arts Institute, honoring the British ambassador tonight, would trade two visiting buyers from Kenosha and one struggling sculptor to the Walker Art Center for a diamonded dowager from Minnetonka, plus one overage art patron to be named later.

Mentioned in most of these transactions is Mayor Arthur Naftalin, whose name, like Zoilo Versalles', comes up in all of the trade speculation. And, like Zoilo chasing an easy ground ball, Naftalin is going to spread himself around. His office tells me the mayor will greet the ambassador at lunch, and two hours later greet him again when the ambassador calls at his office. Theoretically, they ought to be able to solve most of the world's troubles at the first meeting, but neither the mayor nor British diplomacy operates comfortably that way.

Later, the mayor will dine with the group honoring Mrs. Johnson, call on the ambassador again at Dayton's and then head for a meeting on the city's north side, where the disorders have been mild compared with the mayor's tour of all the galas in town today.

But I'm sure Mrs. Johnson will handle the stress and confusion with the easy grace we have come to expect of her. Nor do I expect any of her sweetness to wane when she greets Mrs. Harold LeVander. Oh, true, Mrs. LeVander's husband did accuse Mrs. Johnson's husband of having inflicted a great deception on the people and having turned the country into a nation of political agnostics. But I expect Mrs. Johnson to dismiss this with a "boys will be boys" buoyancy and to view the whole thing with the politically forgiving attitude for which her husband is justly renowned.

She is, of course, in the company of two other gracious women, Mrs. Freeman being the wife of a formerly prominent Minnesota politician who left the state for the serenity of being secretary of agriculture; and Mrs. Humphrey being the wife of the well-known radio announcer.

We are delighted to have them all back and know Mrs. Johnson will forgive us, in view of the Nicollet Mall construction, for extending her the keys to the city in the cab of an idling bulldozer.

One Way to Oblivion

OBLIVION, S. D. — Here in the heart of the billboard forests and the junk shop jungles of the Black Hills, man has spawned the ultimate triumph of American tourism — a railroad ticket to Oblivion.

Critics of American railroading have contended for years the industry is going nowhere. We have here some tangible evidence that the critics may be right. Possibly you read a week ago where the strike-snagged railways could not take you from Minneapolis to St. Paul but could take you, at no extra fare, to Oblivion. It is not quite clear whether this is a commentary on the railroads or on South Dakota.

Unsurprisingly, you will not find Oblivion on the road maps or in the postal guides. And yet it exists, taking its place beside such imperishable Americana as Embarrass and Ball Club, Minn., and Bowlegs, Okla., through which you have to go to get to Maud.

Oblivion, quite literally, is nowhere. Somebody, however, in a moment of cosmic inspiration decided the halfway point in the Toonervillian 1880 tourist railroad between Hill City and Keystone needed a name.

I find it irresistible — the concept of a sweat-soaked highway tourist, up to his gullet in the goofy and garish advertising of the Black Hills roadstand promoters — stopping the car and heading for Oblivion just for the hell of it.

I was not disappointed, therefore, that all there was to see at Oblivion was a little siding where the trains pass between Keystone and Hill City, some uncut grass, a cabin of uncertain origin and some scraggly ponderosa pines.

What else would you expect in Oblivion, a Jaycees' cleanup drive?

Nor was I disturbed that the ride ($2.75, round trip, Hill City to Keystone, treadmilling at Oblivion) is overrated and overpriced, following the familiar pattern of the Black Hills sideshows that include reptile gardens, gold mines, fishing galleries, and passion plays.

Almost everything in the Black Hills is oversold except what was providentially put there, the mountained placidity and the grotesque excitement of the Needles, the oldest rock on earth.

The traveler may enjoy the hills, but he needs ingenuity and stamina to do it. The pity here is that thousands of tourists come away from the Black Hills convinced vaguely they have been had by a breed of pine-coned carnival hawkers, and generally they are right.

I didn't want to take that huffing little steamer into Keystone, for example, because here unquestionably is the garbage dump of American tourism. Here you are surrounded, cornered and routed by billboard announcements in batteries and squadrons; buzzed by helicopters flying tourists to the Rushmore faces, depressed by the tanktown itself and finally convulsed by the unsurpassable pitch of the operators of the Rushmore tramway in the valley who advertise — "restrooms on the mountain."

A man truly has to admire sculptured beauty to exercise that kind of patience and discipline, his fate less dependent on the guidebooks than on a good set of kidneys.

Loudspeakers scream hillbilly music at you at 7 a.m. across the water of Sylvan or Sheridan Lake. The state of South Dakota, which controls the land, has some familiarity with atrocities of the past but with nothing as pathetic as this.

I bleed a little for that, partly because I am fond of the calm and fragrance of the inner hills and admire the genuineness of the western character. But a bullhorn on a mountain lake is like P. T. Barnum in the pulpit. I'm sure I can stand Johnny Cash or Roger Miller at 6:30 in the morning but the question is: Can the prairie dogs?

Eight Million Swedes Reverse – All at Once

STOCKHOLM, Sweden – Where else but here, where the sun shines at midnight, would thousands of people eagerly and gaily drive straight into a three-hour traffic jam – and queue up for miles just for the privilege?

It was Barnum and Bailey on the Baltic.

I don't mean it was violent and disorderly. Visiting experts here for the Swedes' historic switchover from left-to-right-hand traffic were awed – and some were appalled – by the efficiency and discipline with which the Swedes reverse directions.

Visiting experts from Minnesota, of course, are accustomed to it and were not surprised.

But even the resident experts did not expect the Swedes to make a street-filling, sidewalk-jamming, sausage-eating carnival out of it in downtown Stockholm Sunday.

They came from everywhere: out of the fjords, out of the butter churns, out of their air-conditioned saunas. You cannot believe the dimensions of the 4 p.m. traffic snarl in the heart of Stockholm. It was as though the ball game at the Met, the State Fair, the day shift at Honeywell and the Municipal Liquor Store in Robbinsdale all let out at once.

It was a psychologist's field day. Less than 10 years ago the same festive souls had voted nearly 80 per cent against the idea of switching to the right side of the road. And so there was something Orwellian about how the government had them celebrating in the streets yesterday, so anxious to try the new traffic system that thousands of them parked outside the city limits for hours, waiting for the 3 p.m. go-ahead to drive on the right side.

Irresistibly, the Swedes rolled down the main arteries into town. They did not come very fast, because the speed limits were reduced, but they did come resolutely.

The pedestrian multitudes were waiting for them on the squares, in the parks, and along the sidewalks as they did for Lindbergh in Paris and MacArthur in New York. It was one of the epic days in Scandinavian history, standing alongside Leif Ericsson's discovery of America and the founding of Lindstrom-Center City.

It is doubtful that Sweden ever will be the same, or the motorized world for that matter, since the switch reduces the number of major Western centers where left-hand driving is still practiced to England, Ireland, Iceland, and isolated pockets in Richfield and Eveleth, Minnesota.

Foreigners were surprised when the opening-day accident rate here was so low, that no fatalities were reported, that the traffic was so well controlled despite the congestion and that 8 million Swedes changed directions overnight without winding up in the Gulf of Bothnia. But the supremely confident Swedish bureaucrats were not.

They had planned this for four years, and nothing discourages, deters or surprises a Scandinavian bureaucrat. The government's forecasts were right on the money.

There weren't many serious collisions.

The new signs worked.

The people were well indoctrinated.

Even the horses went right.

And the first violator of the right-driving rules turned out to be a Norwegian truck driver who never heard of the change – just as the government predicted.

It had forecast sly Swedish-type schemes to exploit the switchover and this materialized early when a housewife called the authorities saying her husband claimed he was stranded 150 miles from Stockholm Saturday night and was unable to get back until morning.

Sadly, the authorities advised the lady it was not a bad alibi, and it was better than the story about staying up with a sick lumberjack in Norrfjarden, but it wouldn't quite stand up.

I'm not suggesting that everybody got through the momentous weekend unscathed in Stockholm.

My insurance companies and loved-ones had advised me not to ride in all of that curb-to-curb traffic. But there was no other way to learn whether the sudden switch from left to right was going to be traumatic for the average Swedish driver.

By blind luck, I drew as a driver for this clinical exercise one Karin Persson, a 23-year-old University of Stockholm coed who speaks English and who had been driving for three years without an accident.

Miss Persson was lovely, engaged, and insured. With aplomb she slid behind the wheel, appraised the waves of motoring merrymakers driving by her, reflected momentarily on her months of preparation for this hour, and smoothly drew away from the unfamiliar right-hand curb outside the Hertz office.

Inside of 35 seconds she had smashed into the rear end of the car in front of us.

There was a moment of silence, after which I would have sworn I heard from the seat next to me the Svensk version of "Aw, shoelaces."

"Miss Persson," I said, "I do not think we should be dismayed, even though at the moment the driver of the 1962 Opel ahead of you is angrily stepping out of his car and appears to be waving a spear."

Chivalrously, I stepped out of the car and was prepared to be immortalized as the innocent victim of some new Scandinavian epic when the driver looked at his rear bumper, observed there were only a few small dents in the upright bar and generously waved us away.

Miss Persson was astonished.

"A Swedish driver," she said, "when he finds his car is damaged, will either sue you or shoot you. This is an amazing display of fellowship — the man leaving that way without even asking you for your credit rating."

"I don't know about you," I observed, "but after one night in the clubs in this town my credit rating at the local Svenska Handelsbanken is down to zip. Besides, in the United States we get bigger dents from parking lot attendants than the one you gave the Opel."

Miss Persson was now fully at grips with the marvels of driving on the right side of the road. She didn't have six inches of maneuvering room in any direction, the traffic was that thick, but in the inscrutable Scandinavian manner, she was handling it.

"It was so very, very strange," she said. "I want to keep pulling over to the left all the time."

"Try," I interrupted her, "to dismiss those thoughts as quickly as you can, because there is a very large bus heading up the left side."

We edged through the gaily mantled shops of the Kungsgatan, swung clear of the traffic near the Skansen folk museum and into the open at a comfortable 25 miles an hour.

Recalling my experience with a woman taxi driver in the morning, Miss Persson and I spoke English. I tried to direct the taxi driver in the native language, instructing her to head for the Parliament building 10 blocks away.

"Sveriges Riksdag," I said very Swedishly.

We were 15 miles toward Malmo before we got a translation.

Miss Persson was now driving serenely but obliviously. "Haven't," I asked, "we seen this fjord before?"

"They have fjords in Norway," she corrected. "What you see is the Saltsjon, part of the Baltic. But I must tell you now I am rather excited because we are on a street where my fiance lives and it is strange traveling this traffic circle in a different direction."

You must be aware of the new peril here. Miss Persson was lapsing into an airy, lovesick reverie while moving the automobile in an unfamiliar direction through a crowded traffic circle.

You can build the odds just so high before somebody is going to knock you into the lindens.

"Perhaps," I suggested, "I should drive for a while."

Miss Persson relinquished the wheel, set me in the appropriate direction and, in the fashion of women motorists universally, began quarterbacking the whole show immediately.

"Keep the gear in second here, and don't edge too close to the white line," she said. When it got tense, she slipped into Swedish.

The situation was now serious. I was driving a strange, floor-shift automobile in a strange country whose signs I couldn't read. I was in the middle of some kind of schizophrenic traffic changeover, and I was listening to driving instructions I could not understand.

It was aggravated by the young women volunteers who were controlling traffic on each corner. They had the classic Viking voluptuousness, the only difference being that their skirts were shorter Sunday than they were in the days of Thor.

"Miss Persson," I said, "in the face of all these distractions, I'm either going to call the automobile club and ask for a tow or stop for some local tranquilizer. What do they use here?"

"It is the same as they use to cure everything in Sweden."

"And that is —?"

"A plate of pickled herring."

We Lead the League in Stolen Plaques

We now have embarrassing proof that what Calvin Griffith needs more than an accountant is a house detective.

You must have heard by now the first fragmentary reports of the Great Met Stadium Heist, last night's theft from the upper left field deck of a plaque honoring the seat into which Harmon Killebrew allegedly hit his all-universe home run the other day.

The Twins proudly erected the plaque Tuesday afternoon in an elaborate ceremony at which Calvin vowed the seat would be permanently retired, at his personal expense if necessary, and the site never again to be desecrated by anybody's squirming fanny.

Killebrew himself was enlisted to perform the ritual, modestly wielding a screwdriver and hammer on Seat 9 of Row 5 in Section 34 in this ultimate triumph of the publicity agent's art – the Hall of Fame immortalization of one of Calvin's $1.50 seats, a sunstroke special.

So far as my sleuths are able to determine, the plaque lasted six hours. It takes a special kind of audacity, or an extremely high-speed screwdriver, to steal a very obvious and freshly painted white and black plaque in full view of 14,403 people.

The first conclusion is that instead of retiring the seat Calvin should have retired the watchman.

In the face of this latest disaster, the Twins' security office has assumed a characteristic pose and appears routinely flabbergasted. The first move was to blame it on a couple of kids. But I ask you, are you going to be satisfied with these speculative crumbs or are you going to settle for nothing less than an investigation by the ax-flourishing alderwoman, Mrs. Elsa Johnson?

In other words, when it comes to indicting the potential burglar, your candidate is as good as the Twins. Being an orderly hawkshaw, you first will work up a list of suspects.

Might it have been Griffith himself, consumed by the flames of conflicting passions? On the one hand he wanted to see an admired and productive employe honored. In the other hand was the prospective bill for this undertaking – the price of the seat, Harmon's bargaining power next winter . . .

Yes, Calvin's name must be on the list. Then there is the

mayor of Bloomington, still brooding over indignities suffered at the hands of the rabble council in Minneapolis. Have they checked his glove compartment? Or how about Lew Burdette, who pitched the historic ball that the Twins later discovered "would have gone 520 feet" if uninterrupted by Seat 9?

Or have you considered one Paul Libby of 1670 Skillman Avenue West in Roseville, who owns title in the fall to this very seat as a Viking season ticket holder? By a quirk of coincidence, I was contacted earlier in the day by (a) the Vikings and (b) Mr. Libby, the burden of their conversation being: "What in hell are the Twins doing with our chair in left field?"

"My objection," Libby announced, "and this is no reflection on the Twins, is what the plaque would do to my sacroiliac in the fall. Like anyone else I have experienced from time to time a pain in the seat, a twinge in the seat and a crick in the seat. I have never, however, had a plaque in the seat."

"It is," I acknowledged, "an uneasy place to experience a plaque."

The Vikings as co-tenants take a pardonable interest when Calvin's carpenters start pulling out seats that the Vikings sell for $40 a head on the 35-yard line, from a pavilion the Vikings built at a cost of $1 million plus. The news usually reaches them obliquely. This lack of communication has a long and lamentable history, dating back to the Bert Rose regime as Viking general manager. In those days, the Vikings not only did not talk to the Twins but — with Rose as manager and Van Brocklin as coach — the Vikings did not talk to each other.

And so, each of us may have to conduct his own inquiry into this brazen theft. I can only remind you to be grateful for the small good fortunes — that the grandstand is bolted down and Billy Martin's pants are securely belted.

How to Avoid Scenic Saddle Sores in the West

NOTE: The American West is an intriguing blend of mountains, mythology, and sagebrush merchandising. It has some snares for the tourist, but it still exerts a powerful draw on the summer traveler. The writer, who has toured the West annually and climbed in it occasionally, here opens his travel bag as a guide for the novice western visitor.

Historians maintain that the Western mystique—the lure and conquest of the frontier—has shaped the American character as we know it today, and invested it with hidden reserves of stamina, well-regulated kidneys, and resistance to saddle sores.

All of these qualities are still intimately in demand among Western travelers, a situation that permits the modern dude to identify himself gracefully with the old trail-blazers.

It follows that to get maximum enjoyment out of a Western tour the highway wranglers of today must extend themselves, must put themselves in places and positions where they may modestly test their powers of endurance and ingenuity and their ability to withstand a little pain.

The first such opportunity on the long and stimulating run from the Twin Cities to western Wyoming is on the approach to the Black Hills in South Dakota.

(I'm sure you will understand that the traveler follows highways and heeds signs and billboards that suit his preferences and confirm his biases. I do not contend this is the only way to travel from Minneapolis to the Grand Tetons. It is simply the only way I travel it.)

From the standpoint of speed, comfort, and the varied bouquet of the barnyard fragrances, the best route from the Nicollet Mall to the Black Hills is to turn right off the 10th Street barricade and follow either Highway 7 or Highway 212 into South Dakota through Watertown, Redfield, dropping down then to Pierre, maintaining prudent speed to avoid plunging into the Oahe Reservoir.

There are people who are bored driving the prairie, but I do not happen to be among them. Esthetically, I like the size of it and automotively I like the absence of semaphores, one-way markers and yellow curbing, all of which distract me in the city and occasionally cost me.

Alert motorists will begin to read, 300 to 400 miles away from the Black Hills, first signs announcing the imminent appearance of that novel western South Dakota institution, Wall Drug.

This is the first and still undefeated champion in the art of the roadside come-on form of advertising. It began modestly enough in 1931, advertising free ice water. Model A drivers, spewing steam from their radiators and tonguing their cracked lips after a long hot day on the prairie, began stopping at Wall in squadrons. The place doubled and re-doubled. Today it is the Southdale of the Badlands, aswarm with souvenirs, sloppy joes, giant western figures, clanging western music, regiments of tourists and somewhere, no doubt, a drug counter.

As a milepost on the road to the Black Hills it is either an oasis or an obstacle, depending on your preferences. Without dispute, however, it must surely rank behind the Homestake Mine as the largest repository for gold in western South Dakota.

Without quibbling about it semantically, Wall Drug is a sight – the Fibber McGee's closet of the West. My suggestion, if traveling with family, is to put the question to a vote on whether you want to spend time or money here. Once committed, you almost surely are going to do both.

Drive the Badlands, by all means, where wind and water have tortured the earth and left it a lifeless amphitheater of sand castles and crumbling towers painted in the shifting hues of mauves, russets, and beiges.

It is a suggestion of what might happen here if they don't stop fooling around with the water pressure.

If you're camping and heading into the hills, wherever feasible or unless you have sound recommendations, stick with the campgrounds maintained by the federal government. The water, sanitation and sites will be uniformly good, and you can always vote for a new administration if you have a lousy time. In the Black Hills the better ones include the big complex around Pactola Reservoir, Sheridan Lake and several smaller ones in and around Custer State Park.

My favorite campsite, however, is a tiny area four miles up the Roughlock Falls canyon near Savoy in the Deadwood region.

It has only a handful of sites but it is splendidly remote, a short cast from a saucy little creek and walled on all sides in a redstone canyon.

The temperature outside my tent at 5:30 a.m. six days ago, incidentally, was 40 degrees— which may not be a record but is certainly an impressively round number in late July.

If traveling with kids, you will look for distractions where you can stop in conscience and without risking bankruptcy. On the edge of Rapid City, off Jackson Street, there is a remarkable children's playground and fairyland maintained by one of the city's service clubs and its businesses. It's free, but it is good enough to charge at least $2 admission.

If possible, avoid the major highways from Rapid City into the hills and get onto an inconspicuous asphalt route called the Sheridan Lake Drive, Highway 328. After a short jog through ranchland it will carry you 20 unmolested miles into the heart of the hill country, with a little whitewater brook running escort and rock walls flanking the road. In some places it is very close to being subdued alpine, which is not a bad style or period anywhere.

It comes out near Sheridan Lake and opens whatever avenues you want to take from there — trail rides at Gordon's Gulch for $2 a head (truly worth it for the kids), fishing, camping, swimming or boating on Sheridan Lake, auto rides through the hills or sign-and-billboard ogling at Keystone.

Head into Wyoming via either Spearfish or Custer, passing the archly-fluted skyscraper of rock, the Devil's Tower between Sundance and Moorcroft. There is a prairie dog town at the foot of the tower, and it is a charmer.

Drive through Gillette and onto the freeway to Buffalo if you must. I prefer the pre-jet Highway 14-16 that puts you into the red-earthed buttes in solitude, riding the old stage routes. There won't be many trees, but you and your companions may take turns sitting in each other's shade.

The high Bighorns bisect Wyoming outside of Sheridan and Buffalo, lift you onto a giddy plateau and lower you into the superb deep-etched canyons of the Ten Sleep or Shell Creek, and eventually steer you toward Yellowstone or the Tetons.

There are bear men, burro men, buffalo men, and porcupine men. I do not happen to be a bear man and I have latent fears of being pushed into the Yellowstone River canyon by surging masses of merrymakers. I prefer, therefore, to make the highway loop in Yellowstone, take my annual picture of Old Faithful, make my annual explosion at the bear-feeders and then drive to the sanctuary of the Teton Mountains.

If you like the West, and have not visited here before, you are out of your mind to continue avoiding it. True, there are autos by the thousands traversing the valley highways of Grand Teton National Park daily in summer, but the people magically disappear the moment you get off the road and onto the mountain trail.

You may hike, trail ride, climb or crawl, but allow yourself a luxury and go into the mountains. Few national preserves have been maintained as faithfully as this, for which the government and the Rockefellers probably share equal credit.

Unless you expect major inheritances in the near future, I suggest you avoid the swank Jackson Lake Lodge, built with Rockefellerian tastes and price tags. Also avoid the big camping multitudes at Colter Bay, if possible. This does not leave much left, because the Rockefellers manage both.

Eight miles out of Jackson, however, is a campground gem on the flanks of the Gros Ventre mountain range in Curtis Canyon. It has no laundromat and therefore is shunned by most.

Go there. A site will be open, and you may have head-on views of the Tetons. The only thing it lacks is noise.

The Premature Immortalization of Bud Grant

The least one may conclude from the Vikings' lamentable performance Sunday is that the club has now achieved an orderly transition from the Norm Van Brocklin regime to the Bud Grant regime.

This means in just seven years the Vikings have reached that elusive and rare level of consistency whereby they can louse up a pleasant Sunday afternoon regardless of who happens to be the oracle in residence on the bench.

True, there were a few minor annoyances in the club's 42-14 loss to the Cleveland Browns in their final exhibition game. I was disappointed, for example, with the team's failure to find the clubhouse door in time to report for the second half kickoff on schedule.

From time to time I have seen football teams fail to show a workable offense at the start of the second half and some that have failed to show an organized defense at the start of the second half. But this is the first recorded instance of a team failing to show at all for the start of the second half.

My first impulse was to assume that with all of the new provincial influence on the club, the Vikings innocently took the wrong door and were headed for Saskatchewan.

Discarding this notion, I next reviewed events of the first half (the Browns led 28-0), took into account the Vikings' leisurely pursuit of their chores and concluded the worst: The Vikings had not taken the wrong door at halftime and had not been delayed by Grant's oratory but simply fell asleep.

Nobody will want to labor them too harshly for this small lapse. It was an exhibition, after all, and the coach had rather publicly advised the crowd of 40,000 not to expect much in the way of serious football. I suppose you could quibble that almost all of those people were in the stadium with the reasonable hope of viewing at least a few hostile gestures, since they **were** being tapped $5 on the season ticket.

I'm sure that in his breadth of wisdom, Bud knew what he was doing. We shall all no doubt reap the rewards of Sunday's nonviolence with a great, atomic team effort when the Vikings open the season proper against the 49'ers next week.

All we may safely deduce from yesterday is that the Vikings are capable of playing with a high degree of dedicated reluctance. There were times, in fact, when our men functioned with such earnest lethargy as to convince me they were playing the game under protest.

A few redeeming features intruded, however. There had been a good deal of suspense centering on how the newest Canadian emigre, quarterback Joe Kapp, would adapt to the Vikings and the National Football League. As it turned out, all anxieties were unwarranted. Joe blended harmoniously with the afternoon's proceedings by getting thrown for a 10-yard loss on his first play, making all further ceremonies unnecessary.

You should be cautioned, of course, against plunging into any expertise or big money wagers on the basis of exhibition football. Unless you predicted that Ted Uhlaender would hit .260 or that Hank Izquierdo would catch in the majors or that George Romney would be brainwashed by Henry Cabot Lodge, do not bet precipitously against the Vikings at this point; especially since nobody really knows what they plan for the second half kickoff next week.

I say this with full faith in Harry Grant, whose enshrinement locally continues apace to a degree which I am sure must be embarrassing. Thus we read in the Viking program once more: "During his senior year in football (at Minnesota) he played nine absolutely perfect games. His concentration and athletic impulses were so great that he absorbed instruction right away."

And so in the era of a Superman, Superchief and Superscout, we now have the authenticated Super Gopher. When you consider all of that athletic virtuosity, I know it is not asking Bud too much to set the alarm clock next week; and also to allow his warriors the privilege of putting on their G-strings again Sunday in order that they may behave like professionals.

In any event, we are now embarking breathlessly on another football season. The ball club may stumble here and there but it is our ball club, after all. It has convinced us it can fumble around in an exhibition, and we will now sit back to see whether our men can gum it up for money, I mean when it really counts.

3% on the Balance

It is uncomfortable to watch a man making a grab for more money in public, particularly when he is not certain he is being altogether legal about it.

Under certain conditions the consumer will not object too strenuously to having his trousers rifled, as long as the raid is accomplished with a dash of style and savoir faire.

I found this to be the only truly saddening feature of the onset of the sales tax in Minnesota. There are hot-blooded debaters who argue the sales tax is ethically wrong, inequitable and, worse, a nuisance. I would guess most of these judgments probably are correct. My chief objection, however, is that the sales tax – at least in the hasty garments that were slapped onto it by the Minnesota Legislature – is embarrassing.

The legislature set out to construct a new smooth-formula tax levy, but has come closer to producing a blundering pick-pocket.

It's hard to comprehend the reason for all the reckless rush in opening this tanglewood of decimals at the counter within three months of the passage of the bill. The only explanation I can discover is that the state's legislative prospectors, having mined this particular vein without success for years, developed an overwhelming giddiness when they finally put the sales tax over and could not wait until Christmas to get the sack to the assay office.

The state, with a surplus in hand, did not need the money that desperately yesterday. As a result, we are confronted with a mild form of anarchy at the cash register. A visit to three restaurants, three bars, two department stores and two hardware stores yesterday uncovered seven separate forms of cash register and receipt procedure, some of them no doubt illegal.

I found bar owners kicking up their prices 15 per cent on a drink and explaining they needed the extra money to handle administrative expenses, new registers, or prettier bookkeepers. Others explained they needed the money to raise the pay of their bartenders. A few will tell you candidly they do not object to the extra profits. "Anyhow, I think most of us are being reasonable," my favorite bar owner confided. "In other words, the price increases are not exorbitant, even though they may be a little excessive."

I don't think we ought to be unduly harsh with the merchants, who are doing approximately what you or I would be doing under the tempting circumstances. Nor do I think we ought to lynch the Tax Department professionals or even the 100 extra consultants who will be required to interpret the law. The mission of these functionaries is to divine the will of the legislature, an extremely perilous and unrewarding undertaking.

Over the years, in the biblical spirit of charity, the people of this state have adopted a forgiving attitude toward the commuting lawgivers, crediting them with some kind of windy and bungling good intentions. This attitude, regrettably, may be somewhat generous. The legislature's outstanding accomplishments the past four years have been to increase its take-home pay and to reduce the working stiff's.

Accordingly, it grieves me not only to have to pay the tax but to have to peer through 10 feet of smoke at a counter to discover from an illegibly-printed price sheet where the money is going and in what proportions. This casts the cashier in the role of a mess sergeant who puts the private on KP and then makes him squint to read the duty roster.

For these gaucheries and possible illegalities you may consult your legislator. But you may as well stop lobbying. The only thing reasonably certain about the sales tax is that it will be here ten years from now, possibly at 3½ per cent, and 20 years from now, possibly at 4 per cent. The genius of this tax is that its creators make it indispensable. Future legislatures may want to change but will no doubt find themselves in the position of a maiden accosted in her room by a bandit and given the choice of surrendering her virtue or her bankroll. Given the same choice, the state will make the same reluctant decision.

And thus my only suggestion, purely in the interests of your personal research, is to begin today computing the tax in pennies you pay each day, add to that the extra cost on commodities whose price has gone up beyond the tax level, compare your post-tax earnings with your pre-tax earnings, and ultimately subtract whatever break you get on property taxes.

Follow it wherever it takes you — the voting booth, the deposit window, up in the air, down at the mouth, or back to nature. It should be an adventure.

Calvin on the Bridge

Surely you must have concluded by now that Calvin Griffith's rightful niche in history is not the conning tower of Met Stadium but in the Old Testament, somewhere between Genesis and Charlton Heston.

There is something unmistakably biblical about the way this remarkable man has harnessed the weather. He has, in fact, developed these rare, ouija board powers to the point where he is actually able to control such natural phenomena as hurricanes, cloudbursts and mid-summer infestations of chiggers and mosquitoes.

For example, it rained so ferociously at the stadium Sunday afternoon that – if confronted with the same situation – Noah would have called off his carpenters for the day and rescheduled the whole thing as part of a double bill with the tidal waves of Sumatra.

It will be recorded that the torrent did not burst upon us yesterday until (a) it was a legal ball game, (b) the Twins were leading, (c) the Twins had made their daily announcement to Zoilo Versalles that his job was in jeopardy, and (d) with the ball game legal, Calvin was fully certified to cash his crowd of 28,291 at the bank.

Then and only then did the rain engulf us. In this there was simply too much bounty and unqualified joy, plus too much non-returnable cash, for the whole thing to be coincidental.

Transfixed, I observed Calvin's performance at firsthand. I'm not sure you appreciate fully the subtlety and artistic nuances of Griffith's work when he is operating on his highest plane of clairvoyant trance.

The water was pouring down on our people in celestial curtains. There was so much rain out there that Ronnie Kline, if he had been pitching, could have taken something off of his spitter and used it as a changeup.

Panic seized the multitude momentarily. Anxiously, I looked through the windowed partition from where Calvin viewed the arena, as though majestically planted there by C. B. DeMille.

Calvin wears his robes with modesty and tolerance. There he sat, calm in the eye of the storm, fingering his cigarette-holder with one hand and absently playing with his thunderbolts with the other.

On his knee was an attractive child, evidently one of the progeny of the active Griffith clan. This is the other, the warm, the avuncular Calvin. Playfully he bounced her on his knee while dinghies were dispatched from the Red Sox dugouts to rescue the relief pitchers.

You sensed then that somehow everything was going to be all right. The game was 4½ innings old and the crowd was, in the breezy Wall Streetese of the clubhouse, in the vault.

Well, anybody – Phil Wrigley, Tom Yawkey, O'Malley, etc. – can go that far in directing the weather. Alongside Griffith, they are bushers. Thus we had first a 25-minute interruption. The restive thousands get tired of listening to the organ. Unerringly, they wend toward the concession stands, where Calvin is ready with boxes and jars of tempting produce – some of it admittedly a few pennies more this week than last.

This is followed by a second delay, and the crushed thousands in the corridors now become festive. Clearly, they want to cheer and applaud somebody or something. They form outside the crowded restrooms and organize spontaneous rooting sections for those lucky enough to get in.

It is an exhilarating display of buoyant comradeship, of human beings united in common cause. It is raining like hell on the field but they are spending thousands under the dripping eaves and they are eager, foamy and mystically happy.

The sauerkraut is the first to run out, but by now it does not matter. The umpires are churning onto the field led by Ed Runge, who is throwing out an impressive wake as he progresses across the outfield like some determined Mississippi showboat.

Runge kicks out at the ponds with his left leg, then his right leg, a performance which may not be very professional but at least is very aquatic.

You know he is going to call the game but you are not sure whether they will have to beach him to get it done. The umpires are now nearing the right field shoreline, and troubled, look up to Calvin's booth. Friends, I swear it. The water DID part.

'Are You Seducing Me or Refreshing Me?'

Let's be absolutely candid, friends. The most suspenseful part of Sunday's ball-game on TV was whether the brunette in the sarong was going to get undressed in the 7-Up commercial before they switched us back to Halsey Hall.

I make this observation because we have all lived with the vibrating screen long enough now to develop an attitude of detached calm toward the floppy-pants heroics in front of us. In other words, no matter what the narrators are telling us about all that excruciating excitement down on the field, we know enough now to tell a dead turkey when we see one.

There was a considerable amount of this kind of stiff poultry hanging out from the aerial over the weekend, prompting me to give serious thought today to a question from one correspondent who asks: "Truly, now, on most days aren't the commercials really better than the ball game?"

Under normal conditions I would say no. But since sex has now been enlisted by the TV pitchmen with a giddy and galloping exuberance, we really ARE getting more suspense in some of the commercials than in the ball game itself. For example, 7-Up comes at us now with a bedroom-eyed surfwoman who emerges wet and wild from 10 fathoms while tropical rain ardently pummels a 7-Up bottle.

The idea, I'm sure you never guessed, is that we get not only a chance at the brunette but a temporary deed to the neighborhood thatched hut with each purchase of a six-pack. The notion is confirmed when the Tahitian chorus ends its jingle with the line that 7-Up ... "SATISFIES YOU," at which exact time we are given a carbonated closeup of the brunette, with lips half-open, eyes closed and her bottlecap uncovered.

The question is, of course: Is 7-Up trying to refresh us or seduce us?

The suspense comes into it with the time element: Does 7-Up have time to do either before (a) the one-minute commercial is over or (b) Early Wynn comes running out to the mound for the Twins?

Each of the men in the audience must answer this question in his own way and with due allowance for his abilities to be refreshed so quickly. The point is that alongside of this kind of enticement, the ball game frequently suffers when you compare the two purely on dramatic impact.

For example, the only thing I saw to recommend the Twins-Yankee game Sunday on theatric grounds occurred in the ninth inning, when the Yankee infield nearly succeeded in turning a slowly-hit ground ball into the Battle of Stalingrad. Thus we witnessed the pitcher and first baseman colliding without provocation, bodies falling, the ball bouncing wildly and the runner standing safely on first, amazed he had caused all these convulsions.

Confronted with odds of this nature, the Twins' announcing team usually counters with the stubborn, rear-guard commentary of Halsey Hall, who knows that part of his audience is made up of people not entirely attuned to the breezy language of the trade. Halsey therefore hangs onto this group with a comfortably raspy patter that is not only gripping but mysterious.

"Jim Perry has surprised a lot of people by being fast," Halsey will say, "people who used to think he was just another junkie."

Which to the novice raises the question of whether Perry is using liniment or LSD in the clubhouse. But Halsey DOES keep you thinking and thus gets your mind off the occasional dullness on the field. Similarly, when the housewife-fan's interest begins to flag, Hall will rescue the situation with his off-the-cuff jewel of Sunday: "The Yankees may be getting some cheap hits today, fans, but you'll recall that day in California when the Twins cashed in all those Baltimore chops."

This refers to high-bouncing baseballs but, left in this situation, the fan is unsure whether the Twins were playing in a stadium or a supermarket. The confusion properly established, the Twins' announcing team forthwith turned everything over to John Blanchard, for his daily post-game clarification.

John, of course, is the lovable non-announcer who has grasped the announcer's first principle of survival: Do it in such a way as to convince every fan watching that the fan can do it better. This done, you have the audience forever. "There really isn't much I can add," John will tell you, "to this ball game."

Sunday, I would have settled for some simple subtraction.

The Pale-Hearted Padres

We are being burdened now by the pained mewlings and self-serving finkery of former Catholic priests who have discovered they have glands and want the world to pity them and indict their church.

It is not unusual, of course, nor necessarily disgraceful for a man to learn he does not have the stomach to observe an oath – whether he is a clergyman, an attorney, an Explorer Scout or a member of the loyal order of panda bears.

One tends to be bothered, however, by the spectacle of a man commercializing his defection, merchandising his limpness of will and blaming his church for a discipline he did not have the strength to fulfill.

The latest of this breed is one Gabriel Longo, who learned at the age of 30 that his compulsion for girls was stronger than his compulsion to save souls.

Longo left the priesthood in 1956 under the motivation, he says, of the many contradictions within his calling but mostly – to put it bluntly and without the rest of his rhetoric fluff – because of sex.

"You can't hide that within yourself," he explains in the book he is peddling, curiously ennobling the act. "When I knew I wanted sex and without the closed doors or down hidden alleys, I made my decision. I didn't even want marriage at the time because I didn't know love."

Well, better this than to have the clergyman going to dirty movies.

I don't know whether many men have been dragged in chains into the priesthood, but I doubt that Longo was. In a rather specific way he was aware of what his ordination was all about, of the sacrifices of celibacy.

That he could not meet them when the temptations came is no great condemnation. All Longo is – in the most realistic view of the human animal – is just another guy who bugged out. He has spiritual confederates in places like battlefields, baseball dugouts and board meetings.

This might be largely academic except that it is embarrassing to see a grown man whimper in public and to warp his own frailness into a prosecution of his church, and then try to make money on it.

It will be left to the theologians, the pope and history to say whether priests ought to marry, or whether the Catholic church is going to revise this practice soon or ever. One cannot say what this might mean to its parishioners, but I doubt it would mean much. Most young people and married couples are getting enough sex education today from the forums, schools, newspapers and television commercials without having to get it from the clergy.

Moreover, the church's pulpits, I would guess, are full of people who can be practical, tough-minded and inspirational guides to their parishioners whether they are married, as in the case of non-Catholic clergymen, or not married.

In this connection I think the Rev. Francis Fleming of St. Olaf's Catholic Church in Minneapolis deserves somebody's gratitude for telling his congregation the newspapers are not being anti-Catholic for publishing material about priests' defection. Any more than they are anti-Lutheran for talking about the Lutheran Brotherhood hysteria of two weeks ago.

Father Fleming's church is changing, of course, so much so that I'm advised there is less Latin spoken in the Catholic Church today than in the Twins' clubhouse.

The Pumphouse Prophet Flubbs One

On the morning of Sept. 30 the Minnesota Twins stood on the brink of winning the American League pennant. With rivals stumbling over themselves blowing their chances, the Twins could hardly avoid winning. And yet – the anxious thousands were not sure. Except for one.

There was tension on Tenth Street and shaking on Cedar today, but from his glazed-brick pumphouse in the very shadow of Metropolitan Stadium, the man who has become the conscience of the Twins raised a steadying hand:

"Friends," he said, "it don't matter what happens in Boston today or if nuthin' happens in Boston today. You got nuthin' to worry about."

There was a cigar in his face, a dusty black felt hat on his head and a length of summer sausage in his brown paper bag. Like a grizzled groundhog, he emerged from the stadium outbuilding where he has been homesteading undercover since last Monday – the first in line for World Series tickets.

"I don't know what everybody in town's been stewin' about," Ralph Belcore said. "You lose a ball game here last Wednesday, and everybody gets stomach pains. The Weather Bureau puts out a rainy forecast in Boston this morning, and everybody gets hysterical.

"Friends, relax. I been at this for more than 20 years. I told them here Wednesday the White Sox would be the first to go. Imagine them blowin' like that first in Kansas City and then last night in Chicago – my own home town.

Belcore is a 52-year-old electrician's helper who has been squatting at the stadium since his fateful decision nearly a week ago that Minnesota was home free in the pennant race.

"What decision?" he said. "You got three big strong pitchers and three big hitters in Killebrew, Allison and Oliva. I knew the White Sox ain't gonna do it, and I don't like Detroit, and Boston is too damn far away, besides which I don't like the foreign language they talk at Fenway Park.

"So one way or another, it's the Twins in the Series. I got this one by the short strings. I got a rival in Brooklyn to see who lines up first at every World Series. A guy named Schneider. He may be in Detroit, and he may be in Boston, but he ain't in Minneapolis and it's a good thing because there ain't room in this little pumphouse for both of us."

Belcore meticulously distributed his cigar ashes with the flick of a chubby forefinger, sweeping the residue from his rumpled gray coat onto a hunk of cardboard on the floor.

"A man gets to know something about a town hangin' around the stadium nights like this," he said. "Sometimes I sleep outside. Sometimes I don't sleep, but what in hell goes on in this Minnesota Room inside the stadium when you got people banquetin' there?

"I stuck my head in there before a game a couple of days ago, and they was throwin' cold cuts around the room and wanted to know if I needed a drink. I told them if they kept throwin' cold cuts around like that I needed a sausage grinder more than a drink.

"I was takin' my meals for a while at the Thunderbird Motel here, but I ain't got all that much money. Still, I was leavin' the girls some tip money. There were guys travelin' through there leaving 15 cents for a $2.50 lunch but me, I go first wagon on the tips and I'm eatin' summer sausage tonight, brother.

"The only trouble is, I forgot my parrot knife at home."

This gave the visitor pause. "Maybe you mean paring knife," he said.

"Paring, parrot, I didn't have it so I had to forget about finessing the sausage and just ate it in quick bites. I usually eat backwards out here, starting with a couple of ice cream bars and going to a banana before settling on the thuringer.

"The cold don't bother me. We had 29 above one night at Yankee Stadium. I would rate the outside sleeping here pretty good at Metropolitan Stadium, except you can have all those goddamn airplanes.

"I went downtown the other night when everybody said I musta gone to Detroit. Just wanted to see the town. I mean, it wasn't any big deal, the Coney Island joint and Plantation Pancakes, but at least it broke up all the airplanes."

Belcore buttoned his topcoat against the early morning breeze.

"Don't forget, I was the first to say the Twins when it really counted.

"You guys are home free, friend."

One-Third Share for HHH?

The latest advice from the Twins' countinghouse indicates a proposal is now before the athletes to vote a one-third share of second place money to Vice-President Humphrey.

My informant tells me the players who voted against granting a part share to former manager Sam Mele are mortified at being exposed as chiselers and are now seeking to make amends. They reason that Humphrey was with them for at least a portion of the season and, unlike Mele, who stumbled around with them during the nondescript days of April and May, Humphrey jumped vigorously and loyally into the radio booth at almost the precise moment the Twins moved into first place.

"It was really an amazing coincidence," a Twins veteran recalled. "We beat the White Sox one day to move into first and there was Mr. Humphrey with the photographers and all, and it was really funny seein' ole Cal Ermer get jostled into that basket of dirty towels because there wasn't room for him in the picture with Mr. Humphrey.

"And ain't it funny that Mr. Carneal can sound so pleasant and professional when you just know he wants to brain that Mr. Humphrey for puttin' on a minstrel show with Mr. Hall.

"For all those reasons plus the fact that Mele was a lousy bum who didn't play me even though I was batting .190, I think the ball club ought to be generous with the people who were really with us when it counted. I mean when all the TV cameras were there."

On this, of course, I want to observe a strict neutrality. I'm not sure the proposal is really before the Twins, but I'm absolutely certain Mr. Humphrey would decline.

The subject of the Twins lingers, however, with this week's procession of soap-operatic revelations of their frailties and financial frigidity.

We must believe the organization deserved a happier fate than to finish second in this most theatric of all baseball seasons — and then to have its pin-striped demi gods grub out a few hundred extra bucks per man with a show of niggardliness more pathetic than offensive.

And thus I have penned a letter to my good and constant friend Calvin Griffith, portions of which have been authorized for republication by Jim Kaat:

"Calvin, you disappoint me by hanging the horns on Zoilo Versalles publicly. When a baseball team gums up the pennant as imaginatively and monumentally as the Twins did, you cannot pin all of the credit on the lapels of one man. A performance of that scope, Calvin, has to be a full-scale, 110-per-cent, full-throttle, team effort.

"And so now I see you are being urged to trade some of your athletes. Others may retire and still others may have new job opportunities. In one form or another we are faced with the loss of Versalles, Allison, Rollins, Battey, Zimmerman, Kline, Martin, Worthington, Grant, and Valdespino.

"One shudders to think, Calvin, what might have happened if we finished third.

"I know you will resist the temptation to deal away most of these people, partly in memory of your last transaction. As you recall, this sent Mincher, Hall and Cimino to Los Angeles for Chance. It was an exciting trade which, however, ended in a rather classic stalemate.

"Both sides lost the pennant.

"Worse, suddenly we are confronted with gossip-column mush from the club's innermost precincts: Chance can't get along with Ermer; you hold weekly seances with Versalles; this pitcher played the season too fat, and that player played the dollies too hard.

"Calvin, you do not need a catcher as much as you need Abigail Van Buren."

The Saga of Sundown Sidney

Close students of history often have speculated on the fate of Minneapolis if the Jesse James gangsters had not been turned back by the intrepid townspeople of Northfield before reaching their actual target — Vern Gagne's cookie jar and spare change box.

For one opinion on what might have happened, I consulted my personal adviser on Minneapolis police matters, Inspector Donald Dwyer, who said frankly: "Ordinarily, I would have asked the council for 140 more men to handle James. My second thought is that even in 1876 James would have gotten hopelessly lost in the Minneapolis traffic detours and would have wound up either heisting an ice cream shop in Chanhassen or shooting one of our aldermen."

Such is Minneapolis' debt to Northfield, an obligation that spurred me to the comfortable little college town last weekend to view the 90th re-enactment of Jesse's historic raid on the First National Bank.

James lost — again, for the 91st time, extending a statewide losing streak of almost unprecedented length and one that is approached only by the liberals in the legislature.

There are four things in Northfield that must inevitably appeal to the visiting gypsy from Minneapolis, these being (a) St. Olaf College, (b) Carleton College, (c) tranquilizing traffic patterns generally running east-west and north-south instead of over-and-under, and (d) the well-known haberdasher and clothier, Sid Freeman.

Freeman has acquitted himself handsomely in the world since his faltering start when he had the painful distinction of being the only Jewish tackle turned down for an athletic scholarship at Brandeis University.

He now commutes between Northfield and Minneapolis, where he conducts the Skeffington's formal men's wear operations. But it has always been the great frustration of his life that he did not live in the days of the Wild West — or, as Freeman describes them, "the days of the romantic bandits, Jessel James and the Youngelman brothers, Jim, Cole and Bob."

Freeman volunteered to act as my host during the bank robbery festival. I called on him at his clothing store, where the scent of old gunsmoke lingered casually with the lively aroma of matzo balls.

"I wouldn't want it bruited about to my friends in Minneapolis," he said confidentially, "but on Jesse James Day here my intimates refer to me as Sundown Sidney, the kosher cowboy."

Freeman peered flint-eyed over his rack of on-sale blazers, featuring today several check creations in box canyon red and hitching post hazel. For a moment he appeared lost in reverie, as though he had just missed the last stage to Miami Beach. Recovering, Freeman led me onto the street, where thousands had gathered to view the appearance of the smock-cloaked horsemen who would represent James' gang.

"I would have liked to run for sheriff once," he acknowledged, "but gave up the idea as impractical. The county would have had to pin a badge on me, and it just don't have any six-pointed stars in stock."

So here they came, the James' and the Youngers, riding across the Cannon River in their white linen dusters and hitching up in front of the shops where the bank once stood. It since has moved across the street and is now located, by a quirk of coincidence, next to Freeman's store.

They drew their revolvers, and Division Street erupted in gunfire. It was very fascinating and stimulating, although I will have to admit the same kind of drama might have contained more suspense on the Iron Range – where they would have used live ammunition and let the James boys win every other election year.

Later, I consulted an attorney about the possible outcome if James himself had been captured. "He would have gone to Stillwater Prison then," the attorney said, "but today the state wouldn't have got him past the preliminary hearing."

Wurst and Ten in Milwaukee

MILWAUKEE, WIS. – Tenderly and with great feeling, a northeast Minneapolis bricklayer placed a bratwurst wrapper over the passed-out form of a Green Bay Packer fan on a rainy street in Milwaukee Sunday.

It was just a small gesture but at the same time, of course, extremely touching—a display of camaraderie, symbolizing that while the triumphant Minnesotans might have wanted the Wisconsin loyalists to get lumps on their heads, they didn't want them to get pneumonia.

"It was the least I could do for the guy," the Minneapolis fan said. "It's what you call the golden rule. When I'm unconscious like that in the rain, I sure want somebody to think a little about me, even what you call an adversary."

It may also have been the first hopeful sign that the great football argosies of the 1930's may be making a comeback.

For one thing, it made bosom confederates out of H. P. Skoglund, the millionaire insurance man and Viking director, and Stan Mayslack, the bearded ex-wrestler and northeast Minneapolis tavern owner who was a Polish national hero before anybody heard of Yastrzemski.

It also made a number of people broke, including Your Man in Milwaukee.

Ladies and gentlemen, I do not know whether you are familiar with the Milwaukee that used to be before the sociology of the 1960's caught up with it. Much of it is still left, chiefly the part with foam on it.

And so it remains one of the great sanctuaries for the boisterous of heart and the reckless of spirit. It is fraught with German restaurants, and not the ersatz German restaurants to the west, but red cabbage, live-zither, busty-waitressed German restaurants. It also has good food, a sensible attitude toward weekend hell-raising and a stadium where the Green Bay Packers play occasionally.

Into this potentially perilous environment over the weekend rode – from opposite directions and with dissimilar bank accounts – Mayslack's bus tourists from northeast Minneapolis and the aerial odyssey of one Bob Pillsbury.

Both got out without a sheriff's summons, but it was close.

Pillsbury is one of the non-baking Pillsburys, a broker and a jauntily florid man who reminds one facially of Orson Welles before Welles started eating mashed potatoes. He annually sponsors a chartered flight to all University of Minnesota games and extended it this weekend to include both Champaign, Ill., and Milwaukee.

Mayslack operates a scenic bus cruiser now and then. It features non-scheduled football trips and a galloping informality of manner and ticket agentry. One of Mayslack's passengers this weekend, for example, was a factory worker who stayed at Mayslack's joint for one extra beer on his way home Thursday night and wound up the next day in Milwaukee.

"He was dragooned," I protested to Mayslack.

"The hell he was," Mayslack objected, "he was bombed."

Mayslack's entourage paid $67 per person for a weekend that began at 7 a.m. Friday and lasted indefinitely.

"I decided we couldn't afford to take in the Minnesota-Illinois game," he said, "so we stayed overnight Friday in Milwaukee and watched the great struggle between Pittsburgh and Wisconsin instead."

"For scheduling that ball game, Mayslack," one of his passengers sneered, "you ought to give us a refund."

"It gets noisy in the ranks like that," Mayslack acknowledged, "but there's nothin' unruly or felonious, what I mean."

Sports followers will recognize the Pittsburgh-Wisconsin game as one of the great non-epics of our time. Twelve of the bus passengers walked into the stadium when the bus got to Madison. Mayslack stayed in the bus and slept and the other 14 walked unerringly to the nearest tavern to spend the afternoon.

"They were getting themselves keyed for the Packer-Viking game," Mayslack explained, "besides which the Gopher game was on television. Now I know 380 miles is a long way to come to watch the Gophers on television when you can do the same thing in Minneapolis. But there's certain kinds of good fellowship you just can't put a price tag on."

Mayslack's customers, with their roots deep in the asphalt, stayed in the downtown Schroeder Hotel in Milwaukee. Pillsbury's, more accustomed to the uncluttered air of the suburbs, stayed at the distant Leilani Motel — which appeared to be closer to Golden Valley than Milwaukee but at least the walls were thin.

The place also had a swimming pool, into which four members of a wedding party fell in a rather general way around midnight, fully clothed. They began swimming. The motel owner called the police.

"What did you want them to do," I asked, "drown?"

"They weren't from your group," the manager said, "but I regret to tell you they **were** from Minneapolis."

"A very aquatic city," I said loyally.

The itinerary included a continental breakfast and a 10:30 brunch, which began with an appetizer of champagne-and-peach juice.

I bowed out at this point, concluding the drink was probably not only caloric but lethal.

Mayslack's group, on the other hand, opened with tomato juice and Blatz.

At noon Skoglund's party of 10 found itself marooned at the hotel and sent out a distress call to Mayslack's idling bus.

It was a splendid confrontation, Skoglund and Mayslack, both of them world-renowned gourmets from opposite ends of the bank deposit line.

Arm and arm, they sought to walk into the bus together. It was impossible. Skoglund went first.

"It's even an effort," Mayslack explained, "for me to get in individually."

Mayslack bused the Skoglund party to the stadium fraternally and dropped it off at the bleacher gate.

"It was a ball, the game," Skoglund said afterward. "The only thing was that I own part of this ball club, and Mayslack had better seats than I did."

"It doesn't," Mayslack observed, "surprise Mayslack's buddies."